"If you have ever felt unseen or stuck in life's struggles, *Deeply Loved* will meet you right where you are. Reading this book is like sitting with close friends who truly get what you're going through. Bill and Kristi gently remind us that our souls learn to breathe through loving, empathetic relationships with God and one another, and they provide tools that truly make a difference."

Dr. Tim Clinton, president of the American Association of Christian Counselors

"Bill and Kristi Gaultiere have provided an oasis of care in the 'empathy desert.' *Deeply Loved* is deeply informed by both psychological expertise and spiritual sensitivity. In this book you will learn the master gift of humanity: Jesus coming to you with empathy. You will find yourself thoroughly understood and will grow in your empathy for yourself and others. Best of all, you will receive a vision and experience of our caring God that will bring healing to your heart."

John Ortberg, teacher at Become New; author of *Steps*

"*Deeply Loved* is a beautiful exploration of how God's empathy transforms our lives. This book isn't just inspiring—it's practical, offering heartfelt guidance and tools to help you truly experience and reflect God's love in your relationships."

Alli Worthington, entrepreneur; author of *Remaining You While Raising Them*

"We live in an empathy-starved world. And with increased social fractures, we are always being formed to normalize disconnection from others. How do we receive empathy? How do we give it? What does this all have to do with God? I'm immensely grateful that Bill and Kristi Gaultiere have taken the time to respond to these critically important questions. We were created to live deeply loved in this world. But this journey has to start somewhere. What Bill and Kristi offer here is just the place to begin. I highly recommend this book."

Rich Villodas, lead pastor of New Life Fellowship; author of *The Narrow Path* and *The Deeply Formed Life*

"I thoroughly enjoyed reading *Deeply Loved*! Bill and Kristi Gaultiere explore empathy from a biblical and psychological perspective, providing practical exercises to help readers experience and share empathy. This book is essential reading for anyone seeking to deepen their emotional and spiritual health. It will equip you to both receive and give empathy, calm emotional triggers, and manage empathy fatigue. Best of all, it will undoubtedly help you love better in the relationships that matter most to you."

Peter Greer, president and CEO of HOPE International; author of *Lead with Prayer*

"For many years I have benefited greatly from Bill and Kristi Gaultiere's *Soul Talks* podcast. They have been my go-to resource when friends need empathy. I'm so thankful that now we have their knowledge, experience, and research on empathy available in *Deeply Loved*."

Jane Willard, advisory partner at Dallas Willard Ministries; retired marriage and family therapist

"*Deeply Loved* by Bill and Kristi Gaultiere is a well-written, biblically based, psychologically sound, and very helpful book on how to grow in empathy and compassion for yourself and others by receiving God's empathy and love for you. Highly recommended!"

Siang-Yang Tan, PhD, senior professor of clinical psychology at Fuller Theological Seminary; author of *Counseling and Psychotherapy: A Christian Perspective*

"People inside and outside the faith community are crying out to be deeply loved, nurtured, and seen. They are hungry for the heartfelt, healthy, and applicable empathy that Bill and Kristi Gaultiere offer out of their soul-filled ministry. Every page of this book oozes with the empathetic love that can only come from the Lord. Laity, leaders, and practitioners will grow spiritually as they learn from the Gaultieres to love deeply like Jesus."

Barbara Peacock, founder of Peacock Soul Care; author of *Soul Care in African American Practice*

"For much of my life I struggled to be loved—to let love in and just receive. How I wish that during those seasons I'd had Bill and Kristi Gaultiere's newest book, *Deeply Loved*. Here these trustworthy soul doctors reveal our crucial need for empathy as well as how empathy gets deep down inside of us and can flow from deep within us. *Deeply Loved* is a guidebook for your soul that is as powerful as it is practical—filled with experiential exercises, reflections, and meditative prayers. Whether you are learning to open your heart to receive love or learning to be more empathic toward others, this book will deeply change you."

Michael John Cusick, author of *Sacred Attachment*; CEO of Restoring the Soul Inc.

"With deep wisdom, biblical insight, and tangible practices, Bill and Kristi Gaultiere skillfully lead us in giving and receiving empathy for ourselves and others, all rooted in the deep, deep love of God. Beyond cultivating empathy, they are aware of the costs of and even the conflicts caused by empathy. But Bill and Kristi never lose sight of how empathy leads us toward the deep love of God."

Cyd and Dr. Geoff Holsclaw, coauthors of *Landscapes of the Soul*; cofounders of the Center for Embodied Faith

DEEPLY LOVED

Also by Bill and Kristi Gaultiere

Journey of the Soul:
A Practical Guide to Emotional and Spiritual Growth

Healthy Feelings, Thriving Faith:
Growing Emotionally and Spiritually Through the Enneagram

DEEPLY LOVED

Receiving and Reflecting God's Great Empathy for You

BILL & KRISTI GAULTIERE

Revell
a division of Baker Publishing Group
Grand Rapids, Michigan

Published by Revell
a division of Baker Publishing Group
Grand Rapids, Michigan
RevellBooks.com

Library of Congress Cataloging-in-Publication Data
Names: Gaultiere, William, author. | Gaultiere, Kristi, author.
Title: Deeply loved : receiving and reflecting God's great empathy for you / Bill and Kristi Gaultiere.
Description: Grand Rapids, Michigan : Revell, a division of Baker Publishing Group, [2025] | Includes bibliographical references.
Identifiers: LCCN 2025001465 | ISBN 9780800742829 paperback | ISBN 9780800746384 casebound | ISBN 9781493447176 ebook
Subjects: LCSH: Love—Religious aspects—Christianity | God (Christianity)—Love | Empathy—Religious aspects—Christianity | Spiritual life—Christianity
Classification: LCC BV4639 .G375 2025 | DDC 241/.4—dc23/eng/20250404
LC record available at https://lccn.loc.gov/2025001465

The names and details of the people and situations described in this book have been changed or presented in composite form in order to ensure the privacy of those with whom the author has worked.

The self-assessments and psychological insights provided in this book are for educational purposes only and are not a substitute for psychological treatment from a therapist or medical doctor. If you might have a mental health disorder, it's best to consult with a professional therapist rather than a spiritual director or coach.

Cover design by Chris Kuhatschek

The authors are represented by the literary agent Don Gates of The Gates Group.

Baker Publishing Group publications use paper produced from sustainable forestry practices and postconsumer waste whenever possible.

25 26 27 28 29 30 31 7 6 5 4 3 2 1

To the students in our Certificate in Spiritual Direction training program: Thank you for showing people that they are deeply loved by God. It's a joy to follow and serve Jesus with you.

Contents

Empathy Practices

Introduction

If you lived in a city where it was smoggy every day, you might assume it was the same all over the world. You would not know that you were missing fresh air and that was why you lacked energy and were getting sick. You adapted to your situation and made the best of it. But if you moved into the country and got to breathe clean, pure air for the first time, you'd feel like a new person! You'd be rejuvenated and your health would improve. Discovering the experience of empathy for what you feel and need is like breathing fresh air after a lifetime of breathing smoggy air.

We help you begin to breathe the fresh air of empathy by expanding your vision and thinking about empathy, explaining what the Bible says about empathy, drawing on psychological research, and sharing many examples of people we've helped who now say that experiencing empathy has been truly life-changing.

We want you to know that with Jesus you are deeply loved by God (Eph. 1:6). Jesus' perfect empathy for you integrates God's grace and truth. To make this practical we teach you the

Four A's of Empathy, which is our proven four-step process for receiving and reflecting God's great empathy. At the end of each chapter you'll find empathy practices and soul talk questions for you and your friends. Empathy practices combine Scripture, reflection, listening, and prayer to help you trust God's empathy through Jesus, agree with it, and share it with others.

It's our joy and honor to offer *Deeply Loved* for you, your friends, family, work, and ministry. Our prayer is that as you read you will grow in the grace of Jesus' empathy so that you can flourish in your life, love, and leadership.

PART ONE

The Power of Empathy

Empathy is more than a source of comfort—it is also a secret source of emotional intelligence and encouragement that many people miss. As you'll see in chapter 1, empathy is oxygen for your soul.

Empathy is an expression of God's grace. The God of the universe with empathy and love sent his son Jesus to enter our human experience, co-suffering with us to meet us on our level. All of us have been lost and have struggled with lost parts of ourselves. Jesus' empathy finds you whenever you get lost. Your Savior understands your needs, forgives your sins, heals your hurts, gives you flourishing life, and teaches you the great blessing of loving others as he loves you.

But to deeply receive Jesus' empathetic love, mercy, and truth, you need to agree with it and appreciate it. We all have unconscious resistances to the empathy we need. For instance, self-judging diminishes our ability to receive God's empathy and grace. Instead, we need to join with Jesus' empathy by practicing self-empathy. This is the opposite of self-pity—it's self-understanding and self-care in dependence on Jesus Christ.

Receiving empathy enables you to give empathy to others. We show you how Jesus models the Four A's of Empathy that you and the people you care for need. Then we unpack specific examples of how you use these four steps to know that you are deeply loved by God and to share his empathetic love with others.

You'll probably be surprised by chapter 5, which completes part one. We explore the grit and grace of empathy. Empathy is not coddling, as some people mistakenly think—it's empowering. It paves the way for us to receive the truth of God's Word, take responsibility for our life, and grow in Jesus' joy and fruitfulness.

We encourage you to spend time with the empathy practices and soul talk questions at the end of each chapter and share the experience with friends.

1

Oxygen for Your Soul

> And the LORD God formed man of the dust of the ground, and breathed into his nostrils the breath of life; and man became a living soul.
>
> Genesis 2:7 KJV

As a young adult, sometimes I (Kristi) felt like I was suffocating in depression and shame. My soul could barely breathe. What I didn't realize was that my life was void of empathy. Thankfully, I developed my spiritual lungs by regularly asking for empathy from Bill or a trusted friend and processing out loud the thoughts and feelings that had built up in me. Empathy helps me know that I am not alone with my emotions and someone is really there for me. It helps me know that I am deeply loved.

Bill and I have talked with many people who have not received the empathy they needed, especially as children. Their inner self was unknown and unloved, yet they did not know this for many years. That was true for Bill and me.

How do fish know if they are swimming in polluted waters? They've adapted to their murky and unhealthy environment and made the best of it. But if fish somehow find their way into clean, healthy waters, then they'll know the difference. Empathy is like that. You don't appreciate how much you need it until you've been without it, and then someone comes along who is interested to know you personally and reflects back to you what you feel—and you dare to trust and appreciate their empathy as a precious gift from God.

When you have recurring experiences of receiving empathy you will begin to come alive in a new and deeper way. You'll discover what you've been missing and learn how to find other people who are emotionally present and gracious and receive their empathy so you can become more emotionally present to God, yourself, and others. That's how your soul learns to swim in fresh, life-giving waters.

Probably you need empathy more than you realize. It's not just so we can feel better. It helps us to think clearly and smartly. We need empathy for discipleship to Jesus, friendship and family, work and ministry, desolations and consolations, victories and failures, and all the challenges and opportunities of our lives. I don't think I've ever met anyone who enjoys intimacy with God who was not receiving empathy from someone.

The Breath of Life

Our souls learn to breathe through loving, empathetic relationships with God and one another. This was brought home to me (Bill) in a dramatic way as a young father.

An ER doctor was face-to-face with our two-month-old baby girl, pleading over and over, "Breathe, baby! Breathe!"

I couldn't believe my ears. Briana was blue-faced and gasping for air! Nurses were frantically hooking her up to oxygen tubes and putting a heart monitor on her.

Just a few hours earlier I had been holding her at home, and now the doctor was asking Kristi and me if anyone in either of our families had cystic fibrosis. I pleaded with the doctor, "She'll be okay, won't she? I thought she just had a cold. She isn't going to die, is she?"

Briana was taken by ambulance from our local hospital to Children's Hospital of Orange County. We later learned that she had whooping cough, which went into pneumonia, and then she contracted RSV, a respiratory virus that kills a baby a day. It's no wonder she had so much congestion. She was in intensive care for a month. The doctors were afraid she might not survive or would have permanent lung damage.

Kristi and I were also afraid that if she survived she'd have lasting psychological damage from the trauma and pain; we could see her abilities to attach with us and be emotionally present were compromised. She had a bug-eyed and distant look on her face and was slow to brighten up in response to loving attention. In the hospital Briana had to put up a psychological shield of denial and detachment to cope with being hit by wave after wave of trauma in her little body and emotions: tubes in her nose, IV in her arm, alarms waking her, pokes and shots, and a continual commotion of doctors. She kept coughing up phlegm and crying out in pain. Sometimes she arched her back and screamed in terrified rage.

Finally we were able to take Briana home. We gave her respiratory treatments that slowly cleared up her lungs, but as therapists we could see that her spiritual lungs were not healed. *Her soul was not breathing well.* Our empathy inspired us to care for her with prayers, holding, caresses, smiles, and playful babbling. Little by little, her spiritual breathing was clearing up. Her soul was "hatching" with sparkling eyes, smiles, baby talk, and arms reaching out to be held. Right before our eyes we could see that empathy was oxygen for her soul.

Mental Health Needs Today

We participate in an annual Mental Health Collective with one hundred leading Christian psychiatrists, therapists, pastors, and educators to help the church address the growing mental health crisis. Research studies have provided the following alarming statistics among people in America:

32 percent experience an anxiety disorder in their lifetime.[1]

8 percent suffer with major depression.[2]

37 percent more people die by suicide than eighteen years go.[3]

17 percent have an alcohol or substance use disorder.[4]

43 percent need mental health care but are *not* getting it.[5]

If you think these disorders are rare in your church or community, think again. Among the people you minister to, in your circle of acquaintances, and perhaps in your family there are people suffering in these ways who need empathy. To some extent we all have mental and emotional health challenges. In a research study of more than seven thousand people, the average number of emotions that people could recognize and name as they were experiencing them was only *three*: happy, sad, and angry.[6] That means that all their other emotions were unconscious.

Denying our distressed emotions internalizes and hides them in our bodies, cutting us off from the empathy we need to process and care for our emotions and mental health. This drains our energy, leads to unhealthy attitudes and behaviors, inhibits intimacy in our relationships, and stunts the emotional intelligence that helps us succeed in our life and work.

An Empathy Desert

On a Soul Shepherding Institute retreat a pastor named Kit[7] learned about his childhood wounds and exclaimed, "My childhood was an *empathy desert.*" He had just awakened to the reality that he had not received empathy or given it to others. He explained, "I believed that emotions were unreliable and should not lead me in any way. I tried not to acknowledge any negative emotions in my life—I covered them up and repressed them. . . . I did not realize that knowing my emotions, even those that are embedded deep within me, was critical to knowing myself—and even knowing the sin in my life."

Instead of feeling emotions like hurt, anxiety, fear, shame, and anger, he shoved them down and pushed forward. He treated his emotions like a whining child that he did not want to deal with. But denying negative emotions *rejects those parts of you* and diminishes your enjoyment of positive emotions. Kit was missing out on warm and close relationships with people, and he was feeling increasingly distant from the tender love of Jesus.

Negating his emotions hurt his family. He came to realize that he unknowingly taught his wife, children, and church to repress their feelings by constantly giving them solutions rather than being sensitive to their hurts and needs. He admitted, "My wife feels alone. I have not been able to embrace her emotions with empathy and compassion. And my daughter is struggling with anxiety. I have not been giving her a safe place to express herself without judgment." Avoiding emotions had also contributed to conflicts among his staff, which threatened the health and unity of his church. Kit, his family, and his church needed empathy for their emotions.

The Benefits of Empathy

Receiving empathy and giving empathy to others will help you grow in many aspects of your emotional, relational, and spiritual health:

- Intimacy with God and others
- Conflict resolution
- Giving and receiving forgiveness
- Emotional intelligence
- Grit to endure trials with trust in the Lord
- Compassion for the needs of other people
- Effectiveness in work and leadership

What Is Empathy?

What is your understanding of empathy? How would you describe it? You probably have an idea, but for most people it's hard to clearly define. We will be unpacking and applying empathy in the pages to come, but as a starting place, here is our definition:

Empathy is seeking to understand someone's emotions, thoughts, and experiences to help them know they are deeply loved by God.

Empathy combines heartfelt care, thoughtfully imagining yourself as the other person, and using words to describe their internal experiences. Empathy is expressed through a tender heart, soft eyes, curious questions, patient listening, and embracing acceptance of emotions and struggles. Without empathy, we can't be secure and confident. Empathy is a gift of God's grace—even when you feel broken and bad, you are loved unconditionally.

Part of being human is that we need to have God and at least one person breathing life into us through empathy. Thankfully, God has an unlimited supply of empathetic love for us! We can grow in our experience of empathy by practicing with a friend. A first step might be to read and discuss this book together, or you could meet with a Soul Shepherding spiritual director privately or on a retreat.[8]

Empathy as Mirroring

How Kristi and I (Bill) understand empathy has been greatly expanded and deepened by our work as therapists and our study of psychology under the lordship of Christ Jesus. Collectively, we have spent over 100,000 hours caring for people in therapy or spiritual direction. Plus, we've each spent a lot of time receiving therapy and spiritual direction. A good therapist or spiritual director is first and foremost empathetic. This includes heartfelt reflections of feelings and thoughts.

Recent neuroscience research has shown that our brains are wired for empathy with mirror neurons that support our understanding of one another's feelings and thoughts. These mirror neurons fire when we see or hear another person feeling an emotion, which enables us to harmonize with others, feel their emotions, and even experience them in our bodies.[9] The action of mirror neurons amplifies the analogy that empathy is *mirroring another person*. It's attuning to another person's feelings, thoughts, and experiences, and then reflecting back to them what you're understanding. It's listening and caring deeply for their welfare and relationships, especially their trust in God's loving presence and wisdom.

Empathy in the Bible

Early in Pastor Kit's Soul Shepherding Institute retreat he asked, "If empathy is so important, then why is it not in the Bible?" We helped him see that in fact *it is modeled and taught throughout the Bible*, and some of the newer translations of the Scriptures are especially effective at bringing empathy to the surface. The main story on empathy in the Bible is that the incarnation of Jesus as Immanuel ("God with us"; Matt. 1:23) is perfect empathy, and the passion of Jesus to go to the cross, sacrifice his holy life, die for our sins, and reconcile us to God shows us how incredibly far God's empathetic love for us goes.

Let's look at some highlights from the Bible's teaching on giving and receiving empathy (we share more throughout this book, including a summary in appendix 1).

Empathy Scriptures

"You have collected all my tears in your bottle" (Ps. 56:8 NLT).

"Because [the Lord] bends down to listen, I will pray as long as I have breath!" (Ps. 116:2 NLT).

The Lord says, "I hurt with the hurt of my people" (Jer. 8:21 NLT).

"Treat others as you want them to treat you" (Matt. 7:12 CEV).

When he saw Mary weeping, "Jesus wept" (John 11:35).

"Be happy with those who are happy. Be sad with those who are sad" (Rom. 12:15 ICB).

Paul taught, "When I am with those who are weak, I share their weakness" (1 Cor. 9:22 NLT).

"As God's chosen people, . . . clothe yourselves with compassion" (Col. 3:12).

Jesus, our High Priest, is able "to empathize with our weaknesses" (Heb. 4:15).

"Be quick to listen" (James 1:19).

The English word *empathy* is derived from the ancient Greek word *empatheia*, meaning "entering into the suffering, experience, or emotion of another person." It's related to the Greek word *sumpatheo*, which is used in Hebrews 4:15 and is often translated as "sympathy," but the NIV translates it as "empathy." In this verse the meaning of *sumpatheo* is that the Son of God offers us the priestly ministry of empathy or "fellow-feeling with our weaknesses."[10] *For Jesus to have fellow feeling for you means he gets down on your level to feel what you feel and care for you.*

Jesus' fellow feeling for our weaknesses relates to the Greek word *parakaleo*, which means "empathize," "comfort," or "encourage." Forms of this beautiful and powerful word are used a whopping 143 times in the New Testament. *Parakaleo* is what a child who is scared of the dark needs from their parent. It's an essential ministry of Holy Spirit (John 14:16, 26; 15:26; 16:7; 1 John 2:1).[11]

Empathy is related to compassion, a word that is used 117 times in the New American Standard Bible. The Hebrew word for compassion means "womb." To have compassion for people gives them life. *Healthy and helpful compassion always begins with empathy.* Compassion is loving-kindness in action for people.

For many people it's the first word they think of to describe Jesus Christ. But without accurate empathy for the people you're helping, compassion gets off track from their true needs, creates a dependency, and diminishes their dignity by giving them a handout without a *hand up*. Genuine empathy orients compassion and service to meet the true and deeper needs of people. It features an open-minded and softhearted receptivity to people's emotions and encourages them to be responsible.

Being Held in God's Loving Presence

When Briana was so sick in the hospital, I (Kristi) felt all her emotions and was strong for her through her whole ordeal. With my empathetic presence and prayers, I validated her hurts and fears and comforted her. I was determined not to abandon her emotionally. I stayed with her and did not leave her side except when a family member came and took over for a few hours so I could get some sleep. I kept holding her, nursing her, warming her, soothing her with loving touches, looking into her eyes, making baby talk, singing to her, and praying for her during the forty days she was in the hospital.

How did I not collapse in exhaustion from constantly caring for my sick child, absorbing her pain, fear, and distress for so long? Why did I not get discouraged and depressed? It was the empathy that I received from my heavenly Father and Jesus that sustained me.

In the hospital I had many hours each day and night in solitude and prayer. At one point it dawned on me that God the Father felt empathy for me as a mother feeling my baby's trauma. The Father chose not to protect Jesus from suffering in his life or on the cross. I bonded with my heavenly Father as I held my precious, crying baby and meditated on God becoming a vulnerable infant out of love for us. Baby Jesus was needy, his life was threatened, he endured pain and trauma. He cried in the night and needed comfort, and probably he got sick and needed to be nursed back to health. Jesus felt pain and fear like my baby. He was joining with me in empathy and prayers for Briana to keep breathing life into her soul so she didn't die physically or languish emotionally with an insecure attachment.

The power of empathy to heal us and grow us comes from being held in God's loving presence. *The Lord delights in you and sings love songs over you!* It's true. "For the Lord your God is living among you. He is a mighty savior. He will take delight in you with gladness. With his love, he will calm all your fears. He will rejoice over you with joyful songs" (Zeph. 3:17 NLT). Every person is deeply loved like this all the time—even when they reject God. "But God demonstrates his own love for us in this: While we were still sinners, Christ died for us" (Rom. 5:8). Empathy and prayer from someone serving as "Christ's ambassador" helps us to trust God's forgiveness and friendship (2 Cor. 5:20). We come to enjoy the smiles of Jesus Christ so that we are strengthened to believe what is true, serve God, and love people with courage and endurance.

When you learn to ask for and absorb empathy, it gets inside of you, and you will naturally and joyfully want to share it with others. "We love because God first loved us" is how John says it (1 John 4:19 GNT). Love is a big word. If you highlight the empathy in love, that verse reads, *We empathize with others because God first empathized with us.* God offers empathy to us in many ways, like when we pray the Psalms (Col. 3:16) and care for one another as the body of Christ (1 Cor. 12:25–27).

Empathy as Art

Great art reveals God's beauty and goodness in the midst of experiences that are painful, messy, or wrong. That's what empathy does too. The empathy artist enters into the emotional picture of a friend's life, looking and listening. The colored paints in the palette are their friend's feelings, thoughts, needs, culture, history, values, relationships, abilities, failures, hopes, and prayers. The empathy artist uses that palette of experiences to paint a picture with words and nonverbal expressions that illuminate what has been lost, denied, or unappreciated. The paintbrushes include warm presence, listening skills, gentle insights, Scriptures, prayers, and care. Most importantly, the empathy artist's soul is tuned in to Holy Spirit's loving presence and yielded to serve as the Lord's vessel.

Empathy is for all of us to receive and share with others. We normally think of empathy as being for intimate conversations, but it is also an attitude of caring for the welfare of God and people in everything we do—preaching, business, feeding the hungry, talking to a stranger, leading a Bible study, or writing a post on social media. In fact, any work or conversation that lacks true empathy for the people you are serving or relating to is less effective and could even be hurtful.

Jesus is the master empathy artist and we are his apprentices. When you get to see the Lord's picture that brings beauty out of ashes in your life or a friend's, it is glorious! Two people are standing side by side looking into a mirror, and they see Jesus shining through them.

Jesus' Empathy for You

We are likely to miss the life-changing power of Jesus' empathy if we don't understand and appreciate that the Son of God is also fully human. We need to rethink our image of our Lord. Jesus is real. He has human experiences and emotions that are an essential source of his empathy for us. We fail to appreciate the real humanity of the Son of God if we read the Gospels like photo albums of all the shining moments in Jesus' life.

Jesus is not a superhero on a stained glass window. The Bible does not present Jesus that way. If we sanitize Jesus to make him look and smell nice, we don't really know him. Jesus of Nazareth walked dusty roads, got dirty, and had smelly feet. At times Jesus felt lonely, frustrated, and anxious. He had human desires and needs. There were probably days he would have rather relaxed and had a home-cooked meal from his mom than hit the road and encounter crowds running at him, jostling him, and lining up to be fed or healed.

As the "Human One,"[12] Jesus experienced a life like ours with real limitations. The Bible teaches that Christ Jesus, "being in very nature God, did not consider equality with God something to be used to his own advantage; rather, he made himself nothing by taking the very nature of a servant, being made in human likeness" (Phil. 2:6–7). Our Lord chose to accept having limited power, limited portability, limited knowledge—even, in some sense, limited love. He lived in dependence on his Father.[13] Like us, Jesus of Nazareth was tempted to sin and was sinned against. He felt thirsty, hungry, sweaty, bone cold, browbeaten, and soul weary. He experienced sore feet, sleepless nights, pain, irritation, anger, abandonment, anxiety, doubt, and death. He even experienced seemingly unanswered prayer (e.g., Mark 15:34).

Our Lord and Savior's authenticity and vulnerability help us to receive his empathy and to trust him. His emotions make him accessible to us. It's largely through our emotions that we experience life and relate to one another and to God. We can look in the mirror of our Big Brother's emotions to get language for our own emotions. Jesus Christ's empathy for us is a precious gift that is often unappreciated. His fellow feeling for our hurts, stressors, and sins helps us receive his forgiveness, grace, truth, and resurrection life.

Sometimes we feel like a bruised reed that gets stepped on as people walk by. We get hurt, even crushed, by stress, sickness, and sin. But that's not the end of the story: *Jesus was bruised for you* (Isa. 53:5). He sees you and feels for you with empathy. You are the reed he wants. He picks you up off the ground and puts you into his oboe to make heavenly music (Isa. 42:3; Matt. 12:20).

Jesus, you are the Human One and the Lord of all. To be wanted and chosen by you is the best! My soul sings with grateful love to you.

Four A's of Empathy

Kit's lack of empathy had been hurtful to his family and others. Devaluing his emotions led to his struggles with impatience, stress reactions, and being sluggish. It also diminished his intimacy with God. On his Institute retreat we taught him our four-step process to experience deeper love through empathy. He learned to receive empathy from Jesus and to give and receive empathy with his family and others. Later he told us this greatly improved his health, marriage, family, and ministry.

Here's an introduction to our four steps to receive and reflect to others God's empathy:

1. **Ask** questions

   Asking questions is how we learn anything, including empathy. For starters, Kit asked what the Bible taught on empathy and emotions. That led him to ask questions about why he'd been dismissing emotions and how this had impacted his wife, daughter, and others. Then he opened up to others on retreat who were interested to explore his emotions and listen to his heart.

2. **Attune** to emotions

   The members of an orchestra need to tune their instruments to harmonize with one another. Empathy is like that; it's tuning in to one another's emotions. Kit was not in tune with other people's emotions because he was not in tune with his own emotions. On his Institute retreat he started to get in tune because he experienced being in an empathetic community. He was paying attention to his emotions, naming them, feeling them, and verbalizing them in prayer and conversations. Receiving empathy helped him to give it to others. I saw this up close in my office when he worked through conflict with his wife and later with his executive pastor by seeking to understand and care for their emotions and needs.

3. **Acknowledge** the significance

   The big aha for Kit was realizing that his emotions were very significant for his relationships, well-being, and faith. Part of him learning the language of emotions was understanding that his emotions have levels. For instance, he felt *concerned* that his emotional disconnect had negatively affected other people, he felt *disappointed* that he had not learned about emotions sooner, and he felt *very sad* that he had hurt people he loved and missed out on healthier relationships with them.

4. **Affirm** strengths

   It was tempting for Kit to fall into guilt and shame for hurting his family and church with his lack of empathy. The affirmations he received from his retreat community helped him appreciate that he was taking good steps forward by being vulnerable and seeking to learn by doing the empathy practices we recommended.

As you continue reading, our prayer is that you are awakening to how deeply you are loved through receiving and reflecting God's great empathy for you. To help you apply this material, at the end of each chapter we provide four practical steps, an empathy practice, and soul talk questions.

GO DEEPER

To get free *Deeply Loved* resources, receive empathy from a Soul Shepherding spiritual director, or go on a Soul Shepherding retreat, visit SoulShepherding.org /DeeplyLoved or scan this QR code:

EMPATHY PRACTICE:

Breathing with Empathy

When I (Bill) was younger, I often hurried breathless through the day, stressed by trying to accomplish more than I could fit in one day. I did not realize that I was generating anxiety from shallow breathing and repressing my emotions. It was like I was just sipping oxygen all day. Then I learned to use Breath Prayers from the Bible to help me slow down, breathe deeply, feel my emotions, center my thoughts, and savor God's loving presence. This helped me move from an anxious brain state to a healthy brain state.[14]

Probably there are times during the day when you don't realize that you are stressed and your breathing is shallow. Yet, it's God's breath of life that makes you a living soul (Gen. 2:7). Jesus breathes this divine life into you (John 20:21–22). Jesus understands the stress, hurts, temptations, and trials that make it hard for us to breathe free and easy. As our High Priest, Jesus is able to "empathize with our weaknesses" because he "has been tempted in every way, just as we are—yet he did not sin" (Heb. 4:15).

To help you receive Jesus' empathy and breathe with his Spirit, I wrote a Breath Prayer for you that's inspired by Hebrews

4:15: "Jesus feels for me . . . I trust you, Lord . . ." (While writing this book, I have benefited from this prayer and enjoyed praying it for you.) Here's a helpful prayer rhythm to try.

Identify a concern and tell the Lord how you feel about it . . .

Breathe in deeply and slowly . . . Hold your breath . . . Exhale fully . . . Repeat . . .

As you breathe in, pray "Jesus feels for me . . ."

As you exhale, pray "I trust you, Lord . . ."

For a while continue breathing, "Jesus feels for me . . . I trust you, Lord . . ."

You can adapt this Breath Prayer for a relationship by praying, "Jesus feels for us . . . We trust you, Lord . . ." You can intercede for a loved one by praying, "Jesus feels for [name] . . . May she/he trust you, Lord . . ."

SOUL TALK

1. What is one thing you learned about empathy?
2. How do you relate to Kit's story of dismissing the emotions that he and others were having?
3. How do you feel about your weaknesses? How might this be impacting your ability to receive empathy?
4. Which of the empathy Scriptures is your favorite? Why?
5. What was your experience with the Breath Prayer, "Jesus feels for me . . . I trust you, Lord . . ."?

2

Jesus' Empathy Finds Us

> We have a high priest who can feel with us when we are weak. He has been tested in every way, just as we are. But he did not do anything wrong.
>
> Hebrews 4:15 WE

We all long for God's blessing, but often we don't feel it. God may feel far away when you are hurting or struggling. Yet, the truth is that you are not alone—Jesus sees you and has empathy for you. He says, "Blessed are you in your difficult circumstance because my Father's world is available to you." That's his general invitation in each of the eight beatitudes that open his Sermon on the Mount.[1]

Jesus' blessings are not words of sugarcoated reassurance—they are words of grace and truth spoken in your time of need for you to learn by heart and trust as real, even when they don't feel real. What he says to you in his great sermon he says to you as your High Priest: *I feel with you when you are weak. Your pain is my pain. You've been lost and I'm here to find you, heal your sin and shame, reconcile you to God, and teach you how to live from the resources of the Kingdom of the Heavens.*[2]

> *Yes, Jesus, your words of blessing are my lifeline. I receive your forgiveness and grace—I trust in your unfailing empathetic love.*

Lost and Found

One day Bill and I (Kristi) took our three little children to Disneyland. We were exploring Toontown, which is like being inside a cartoon. We were making our way through the crowds to the next attraction when all of a sudden we realized that Jennie, our middle child, who was four years old at the time, was missing! I cried out, "Where's Jennie? Bill, have you seen Jennie? Where did you last see her?" Then everything became a blur as Bill and I ran around frantically asking people if they'd seen our little girl. My heart was pounding out of my chest and my thoughts were swirling in fear: *What if she's been kidnapped?* We found a Disney staff member and asked for help. Soon we heard on the loudspeakers, "Code red! Code red!" Staff everywhere were looking for our little girl. Thank God, they found her! She was in Minnie's House, waiting in line to get her picture taken with Minnie.

Many of us got lost *emotionally* as children because we did not receive sufficient empathy. Perhaps you received little or no empathy from your parents, you went through trauma that caused you to shut down emotionally, or your personality got bent on being self-sufficient and dismissing your emotions and needs.

The obvious side of receiving empathy is that someone cares for you deeply, but just as essential is that you trust that person's heart by asking for the care you need and accepting it. To be found with empathy means you are receiving and appreciating tenderhearted warmth, gentle inquisitiveness, patient listening, validation of your emotions and needs, and grace that loves you as you are. When you receive empathy like this, you feel seen, heard, and wanted. Without it, separated from deeply loving relationships, your true self won't develop well and important parts of you will get lost. There are many parts of you that need empathy, like your emotions, thoughts, needs, values, memories, and dreams. If those parts of you are dismissed by others or denied by you, then they get lost in the dark of your unconscious.

Over the years we've helped many people experience empathy. Often they realize they went years without being really known, understood, and accepted. It's like children in school who have blurry vision but don't realize this until their teacher figures it out. When they get prescription glasses they step into a whole new world! They can read words at a distance, see their teacher's face, and enjoy the beauty of trees, birds, and sky. Receiving empathy from someone helps you see and savor God's blessings that you've been missing. You learn how to access your emotional intelligence, resolve conflicts, and cultivate healthy relationships. *You discover that your true self is deeply loved.*

We find each other's true self by listening with heartfelt interest. "How did your event go yesterday? . . . What are you feeling? . . . Tell me more . . . What do you need? . . . What are you hoping for? . . . How can I pray for you?" Soul touches like these give life.

The Psychology of Jesus' Empathy

While writing this chapter, I (Kristi) was caring for our two-year-old granddaughter Ellie overnight. During the night she got very sick with croup and kept coughing and crying. As I held her, I prayed for her healing and for her to receive Jesus' empathy through me. I tried to comfort her with affection, steam from a vaporizer, water to drink, a snack, and walking. Nothing calmed her down. Finally, I gave her explicit words of empathy with a soothing voice: "You miss your mommy. She loves you so much. She will be with you soon." I continued to verbalize my empathy for her, repeating words like this, and after a few minutes she burrowed her head into my chest. It wasn't that she was worn out from crying and collapsed limp; nor was it that she had to deny her emotions to cope. Either of those responses would have meant part of her was lost, unknown, not attached in loving relationships. Instead, her inner self had been found by my empathy and she was holding on to me, receiving my love, and resting peacefully.

Even as a two-year-old who was just beginning to develop her vocabulary, what Ellie most needed was to be comforted with *tenderly spoken words of empathy*. That restored her base of secure attachment and enabled her to return to peace and joy. The empathy of Jesus that was inside of me got inside of her. (Of course, she didn't know that Jesus was helping her feel deeply loved, but I pray that one day she will.)

There have been many studies on the importance of secure attachment to facilitate psychological maturity, well-being, and loving relationships. For instance, about seventy years ago Harry Harlow, an American psychologist in the middle of the twentieth century, conducted studies of infant monkeys' maternal bonding and shed light on how little children develop secure attachment in loving relationships that help them know they are safe and sound. Infant monkeys were separated from their mothers and put in a cage with access to two surrogates: a wire "mother" that had milk and a cloth one that had no milk. Harlow observed that the infants would go to the wire mother briefly to get milk, but they'd spend all their time with the cloth mother.[3] In a later experiment, infant monkeys who were isolated from maternal care for a year could not recover, but those who were isolated for three months were able to recover if they later received care.[4]

After we discussed Harlow's monkeys during a weeklong Soul Shepherding Institute retreat, Michael shared,

> My mother didn't touch me for the first three months of my life. All through my childhood she was distant. She provided for my physical needs and I always knew that she "loved" me, but she never showed any emotions or noticed any of my emotions. Now I feel uncomfortable when someone hugs me or asks me how I feel. I long to feel held, but it's awkward and embarrassing. My body goes stiff and my emotions go dark.

If you were raised on rations emotionally and your personality was formed in relationships that were emotionally detached or insecure, you may have an unconscious knee-jerk reaction to shut down emotions because they feel overwhelming. When you come to points of having emotion, instead of putting on the brakes, you can learn to choose to feel the emotion and ask for empathy from God or a friend.

When Amber, who had burned out as a missionary, heard about Harlow's monkeys during her training with us, she responded,

> I've always gone to the wire monkey to get my physical needs met, not the cloth monkey who provides affection. For me the wire monkey was my dad who gave me money. It's no wonder that I have never been able to receive empathy from God. Now I know it's because I have to receive empathy from people to metabolize it from God.

This insight motivated Amber to begin meeting regularly on Zoom with a spiritual director on our team. During each session she practiced sharing her heart to receive empathy rather than judging herself to be "needy" as she'd always done in her previous relationships. Her persistent courage to be emotionally honest fueled her growth in secure attachment and enabled her to feel God's empathy for the first time. For instance, sometimes when she meditated on Scripture or prayed in nature, she experienced a sense of God listening to her and caring deeply about what she felt and needed. She received personal healing and renewal, which enabled her to return to her mission work with joy. Three years later she is still thriving.

Amber learned the language of emotions and came to trust that the Spirit of Jesus[5] was feeling deeply for her and caring for her personal needs through her spiritual director.

Learning the Language of Emotions

A research study found that only 36 percent of people could accurately identify their emotions as they were occurring.[6] Perhaps you or someone you care for has not learned the language of emotions. That was my story growing up. I (Bill) was the oldest of five children, and my role was to be the "parentified child" who was highly responsible and helped with my younger siblings. My mother was emotional and relied heavily on me for support. To cope I retreated into my head or got busy. I played sports, did well in school, worked hard to earn money, and was helpful to others. My family and other people had high expectations for me—and I had even higher expectations for myself.

In college I studied psychology and learned that I did not understand my emotions or how to talk about them. I did not know how to receive the empathy I needed. At the start of my senior year, I served as a teacher's aide for Cara, one of my psychology professors. I met with her each week and at our first meeting I announced, "I'm excited to learn from you about being a Christian counselor." She replied, "We can get to that later. Let's talk about *you*. How do you feel?" I almost looked over my shoulder to see who she was talking to! I thought to myself, *How do I feel? I don't know. Why does it matter?* Until that moment I do not remember ever reflecting deeply on my emotions or being empathetically asked about them. I only knew how to talk about what I was doing and thinking.

Cara looked at me with a warm smile and asked again, "How are you *feeling*?" She was curious, compassionate, calm, secure, stable, undistracted, patient. I could tell she was tuned in to my well-being and was emotionally strong to support me. This was new for me. That year, every week when I met with Cara, I would tell her what I was doing and thinking and then she'd say, "It seems you feel anxious . . . frustrated . . . angry . . . discouraged . . . sad" or another emotion. Often I'd reply, "Hmm, I do feel that." Then I'd elaborate. When she felt my emotions, it helped me to feel them too. Her face, words, and tone of voice reflected my feelings and needs back to me. Furthermore, receiving her empathy enabled me to engage Jesus' empathy for me and trust that I was deeply loved by God.

Three-Way Empathy

One pleasant evening in July, Bill and I (Kristi) were having dinner outside on a deck under the large redwood trees with Richard and Nancy, a pastor couple who had come to our Institute retreat on "Soul Care Ministry." Richard was at the end of his rope and found us by searching the internet for help. We listened to him tell us that he was burned out, broken down, feeling like a failure, questioning if he was still called to pastor, and wanting to quit. They had experienced division in their church from the presidential election, the COVID pandemic, and his response of keeping church open and requiring masks. A number of people had left their church and were treating him as an enemy. The two of them had put so much into his training in seminary and giving their best to pastor their congregation. Now their ministry, livelihood, and community were destabilized and they felt alone. They were overloaded with grief, self-doubt, and shame.

I zeroed in on Richard because he was in active crisis. I drew on my emotions from past trials in leadership to help me understand and care for *his* emotions. I attuned to his thoughts and feelings, offering him empathy for what he had experienced.

As I was listening to Richard, I was attentive to the Lord's presence and praying silently. I knew Jesus had deep empathy for him and wanted him to trust this. I thought about the ways Jesus experienced trials like Richard and Nancy were going through. Jesus received judgment and opposition from religious leaders (e.g., Mark 3:1–6). He had to deal with government restrictions (Matt. 17:24–27; Luke 2:1–5). Within the community he led there were conflicts and divisions (Matt. 20:20–28; Luke 9:46; 22:24–27). He was abandoned by many of his disciples after they heard him say things they didn't like (John 6:66). He was betrayed (Matt. 26:14). Much of the time he felt alone, like no one understood him or what he was going through (John 2:24; 7:5; Mark 15:34). When his ministry seemed to fail, he was tempted to feel discouraged (Mark 6:4–5; 15:34; John 6:67). I shared with Richard these examples of Jesus' trials and emotions and suggested, "Jesus feels empathy for you. And Jesus thanks you for serving as a pastor and sharing in his sufferings."

Richard began to tear up. Nancy looked lovingly in his eyes and grasped his hand. *For the first time since his crisis, instead of feeling shame he felt empathy.* He was moving from a posture of insecure attachment to secure attachment.

Three-Way Empathy

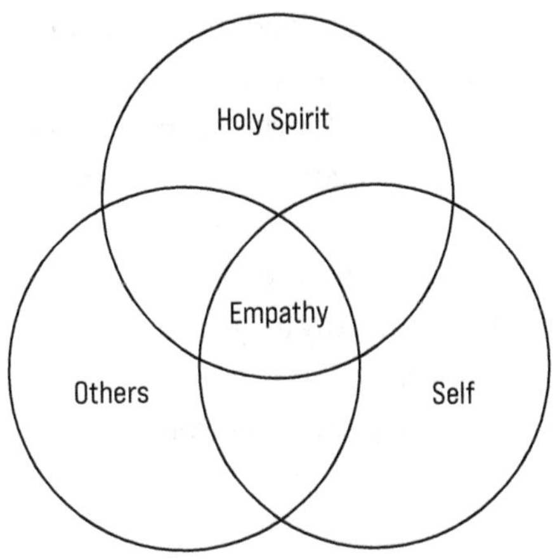

Shortly after their retreat, Richard and Nancy returned to their church and ministry. They wanted to deepen their personal healing and growth, so they enrolled in our online training program to earn a certificate in spiritual direction. Six months later, at their second retreat, their countenances had gone from downcast to bright and joyful. Richard told us, "When you shared Jesus' empathy for me, I had a breakthrough and felt renewed courage to continue in my service to him as a pastor." He was receiving three-way empathy from Holy Spirit, others (i.e., me, Bill, and his wife), and himself (see diagram above). I was honored to serve as Christ's ambassador to mediate God's empathetic friendship to Richard (see 2 Cor. 5:20 MSG).

Three-way empathy is prayerful listening that helps us feel deeply loved by God. That's because when two people agree in prayer, Holy Spirit *manifests Christ's presence* (Matt. 18:19–20). That cord of three strands is not easily broken (Eccles. 4:12). Way back in the twelfth century, Aelred of Rievaulx wrote about the blessing of "spiritual friendship," which was his term for what we are calling three-way empathy. He penned a beautiful line: "Here we are, you and I, and I hope that Christ makes a third."[7] When Richard and Nancy experienced this Christ-led community of empathy, it helped them navigate the storms in their church, repair their weary and torn souls, deepen intimacy in their marriage, and care for the people in their church.

As these examples of people receiving empathy illustrate, often the best way to be helped by empathy is in an explicit context for it, like meeting with a friend or spiritual director who is experienced at giving empathy in order to minister Jesus' loving presence. *How do you find a friend like that? How would you recognize if someone was a good person to be emotionally vulnerable with?*

Traits of an Empathetic Friend

A good listener who doesn't talk over you or give advice
Gracious, warmhearted, and nonjudgmental
Self-aware and on their own journey of personal growth
Reliant on Jesus to help them be loving

If you don't have a friend like this, then pray for one and look to be that kind of a friend to others. Of course, the best source of empathy and care is the Lord Jesus Christ. Receiving more empathy from Jesus starts with appreciating his tenderness in the Gospels.

The Tender Beatitudes

I (Bill) have enjoyed studying and meditating on Jesus' Sermon on the Mount for many years. I believe the key to benefiting from his teaching is understanding his opening beatitudes, which we introduced at the start of this chapter. Sadly, many Christians have misinterpreted Jesus' beatitudes as advice to engineer their way into getting blessed by God. But Jesus is not telling us to do anything—he's offering us *pure grace*. The blessings he offers us are not from being poor in spirit, meek, mourning, and so forth—they are from being in the Kingdom of the Heavens. In each beatitude Jesus empathizes with the distress you are feeling to shift your attitudes and inspire your prayers. He invites you to place yourself and your circumstances into the wonderful but unseen reality of his kingdom in your midst.

Why do I say Jesus is giving us empathy for our *emotions*? Where are the emotions in his eight beatitudes? The first word in each of Jesus' promises appeals to our emotional well-being: "Happy are you . . . Happy are you . . . Happy are you . . ."[8]

The multitudes who first heard Jesus' happy words of grace largely consisted of people who were suffering, sick, and emotionally broken (Matt. 4:24). They were cast aside as misfits and oppressed by religious bullies and a brutish Roman government. But Jesus felt deeply for them and invited them into his circle. Our Lord loves the down-and-out and all kinds of people, including *you*!

To help you gain a fresh appreciation of Jesus' blessings that bring joy to your heart, I have paraphrased Matthew 5:3–10 as the "Tender Beatitudes." May Jesus' words fall like rain on your thirsty soul.

> Blessed are the poor in spirit who are lacking spiritual success because they can join me in my Father's world.
>
> Blessed are the tearful who keep crying, the shy who feel insecure, and the wounded who have not received justice because they can rely on God's hidden sources of eternal comfort, grounding, and provision for their every need.
>
> Blessed are the empathetic who absorb the pain of others because they can discover that God is always empathetic to them, spilling over with endless mercies and loving kindnesses.

> Blessed are the sincere do-gooders who are unappreciated, criticized, and mistreated because they can see that God is personally taking care of them.
>
> Blessed are the peacemakers who are kind, gentle, and trying to bring harmony in conflicts but are tempted by fear and shame when others get angry at them. Why are they blessed? It's not because of their good works of peacemaking—it's because they have become daughters and sons in the family of heaven.
>
> Blessed are all these tenderhearted people who get mistreated because they can join me in my Father's world.

After I read the Tender Beatitudes of Jesus on a recent Institute retreat, it seemed everyone was feeling the warmth of God's loving presence in a flood of divine empathy. A woman shared with our community, "I come from a tradition of heady theology that preached, 'Study, study, study the Bible!' As I'm listening, I'm waking up to realize that I've missed a lot of the richness and tenderness of the gospel. I feel myself tearing up as you talk about Jesus' empathy and grace. I keep thinking, 'Wow! He really is that good!'"

The Good Shepherd Finds You!

How does it feel for you that Jesus never wants you to get lost? If you place yourself in Jesus' story of the shepherd who leaves his other ninety-nine sheep to find you when you are lost, what do you feel?

> Suppose one of you had a hundred sheep and lost one. Wouldn't you leave the ninety-nine in the wilderness and go after the lost one until you found it? When found, you can be sure you would put it across your shoulders, rejoicing, and when you got home call in your friends and neighbors, saying, "Celebrate with me! I've found my lost sheep!" Count on it—there's more joy

> in heaven over one sinner's rescued life than over ninety-nine good people in no need of rescue. (Luke 15:4–7 MSG)

Often we limit our application of this Scripture to the first time we repent of our sins to be forgiven and saved or born again. Certainly, that is the most important moment of our lives! Yet the Bible teaches that salvation is not only an event, it's also an *ongoing process* for us to work out in dependence upon God's grace (Phil. 2:12–13; Col. 1:21–23). In this life we often have lost parts of ourselves that need to be found, saved, and loved by our Good Shepherd. As we said near the beginning of this chapter, this includes emotionally lost parts. To grow in our intimacy with God includes knowing God more fully and joining God in knowing ourselves more fully. To know more of God but with only a small part of ourselves is not a very intimate relationship. We need to be emotionally found by our Shepherd to help us learn to believe, trust, and apply the truth of our Savior's ever-reaching, ever-deepening love.

David was a man after God's heart largely because he offered vulnerable prayers like, "Search me, God, and know my heart; test me and know my anxious thoughts. See if there is any offensive way in me, and lead me in the way everlasting" (Ps. 139:23–24). Holy Spirit's continual searching for you in Psalm 139 is empathy. It is God's relentless, loving pursuit to find you—with your emotions, wounds, sins, needs, beliefs, and strengths—so that you wake up to be fully present, trusting God and loving others as God loves you.

Jesus' Four A's of Empathy for You

Kristi and I have learned so much about empathy from Jesus. We've studied how he interacted with people in the Gospels to help us develop the Four A's of Empathy. Receiving Jesus' empathy in these ways cultivates your intimacy with God, emotional health, and loving relationships with others. We encourage you to practice these four steps for receiving Jesus' empathy in your prayers and Scripture meditations.

1. **Ask** QUESTIONS

   To receive empathy, ask yourself what you're feeling or ask for empathy from a friend. Jesus is your Friend, and he asks you empathetic questions to invite you to share personally. He asked 307 questions in the Bible.[9] Some of these questions focused on his empathy for people. For example, "What is it you want?" (Matt. 20:21), "What do you want me to do for you?" (Mark 10:51), "Why are you troubled?" (Luke 24:38), "Do you want to get well?" (John 5:6), "Why are you crying?" (John 20:15).

2. **Attune** TO EMOTIONS

   Jesus tunes in to your emotions to feel for you. Seven times the Gospel writers explicitly name Jesus' compassion—it's the most common word they use to describe our Lord and Savior.[10] With compassion, he attuned to the emotions of the widow of Nain who was crying because she had lost her only son (Luke 7:11–16). When Mary's brother Lazarus died, Jesus wept for her (John 11:35). For all of us, Jesus is ready to "empathize with our weaknesses" (Heb. 4:15). What a blessing it is that Jesus feels for you!

3. **Acknowledge** THE SIGNIFICANCE

   Jesus has empathy for the weight of what you are feeling in different situations. When four men cut a hole in a roof to lower their sick friend at the Lord's feet, "Jesus saw how much faith they had" (Mark 2:5 CEV). When he saw that the rich young ruler was holding on tight to many things of the world, "Jesus looked at him and loved him" (Mark 10:21). After Jesus had been crucified and his disciples were so scared and upset, the risen Lord appeared to them and put words to their heavy emotions of distress and doubt, which strengthened their faith (Luke 24:37–38).

4. **Affirm** strengths

Jesus' empathy for you culminates in affirmation. The ministry of giving encouraging words is powerful, especially when it comes on the heels of empathetic questions, attunement, and acknowledgment. Here are a few examples of Jesus speaking words of encouragement to people like us: "You have great faith!" (Matt. 15:28). "You are a rock" (Matt. 16:18 GNT). "You want to do what is right" (Matt. 26:41 CEV). "I chose you" (John 15:16).

GO DEEPER

To get free *Deeply Loved* resources, receive empathy from a Soul Shepherding spiritual director, or go on a Soul Shepherding retreat, visit SoulShepherding.org /DeeplyLoved or scan this QR code:

EMPATHY PRACTICE:

Connecting with Jesus' Emotions

When I (Kristi) get emotionally triggered or stressed, I'm tempted to feel alone and like no one would understand me. I've learned at these times to look into the emotions of Jesus in the Gospels like a mirror. It's like Holy Spirit helps me turn through the pages of Jesus' life on earth and land on one where he felt what I'm feeling. Connecting with Jesus' emotions helps me set my affections on him (Col. 3:1) and feel his empathy (Heb. 4:15). It strengthens me to join with his empathy for other people.

As a sensitive feeler I've been judged and shamed for having so many emotions. If you have read our book *Healthy Feelings, Thriving Faith*, you know I am a shame type on the Enneagram, and it's hard to get shame off me. Before I understood this, sometimes I unknowingly projected the shame I felt for being emotional into Scripture. Bill, motivated by love for me and others who need help valuing their emotions, wrote a Bible study on Jesus' emotions. Not only did I feel loved by Bill because of this gift, but I received God's love for me in each of the emotions Jesus felt. It gives me joy to share this Bible study with you, as I know it will help you and your friends trust Jesus' loving empathy for you.

In this Bible study, Bill identified thirty-nine of Jesus' emotions that are explicitly named in the Greek (see the bold words below). Knowing that Jesus of Nazareth felt so many emotions gives me grace to be more accepting of all the emotions I feel. Of Jesus' thirty-nine emotions (or attitudes that include emotions), Bill designates eleven as core emotions: anxiety, anger, shame, sadness, pain, surprise, hope, trust, love, joy, and peace.[11] Notice that typically the first five feel negative and the last six feel positive.

As you read the list of Jesus' emotions below, try these steps to help you reflect and pray:

1. Ask Holy Spirit to guide you as you read.
2. Underline Jesus' emotions that you relate to.
3. Meditate on Scriptures that speak to your emotions.
4. Pray about a situation where you feel as Jesus did.

Jesus' 39 Emotions

Anxiety

Preparing to go to the cross, Jesus prayed with such great **anxiety** that he sweat drops of blood (Luke 22:44). He also felt **afraid** (Heb. 5:7), **pressured** (Luke 12:50), **troubled** (John 11:33; 12:27), and **terrified** (Mark 14:33).

Anger

Jesus was **angry** with the Pharisees who opposed him healing the man with a deformed hand on the Sabbath (Mark 3:5). He also felt **boiling passion** (John 2:17), **indignation** (Mark 10:14), and **stern displeasure** (John 11:33, 38).

Shame

By choice, Jesus experienced a **shameful** death on the cross for our sins (Heb. 12:2). He also felt **depressed** (Mark 14:33) and **forsaken** (Mark 15:34).

Sadness

From the Mount of Olives Jesus looked down on Jerusalem and wept with **sadness** because they rejected God's offer of peace (Luke 19:41). He also felt **grief** (Mark 3:5), **deep sighs** (Mark 8:12), **deep distress** (Matt. 26:37), **crushing grief** (Mark 14:34), and **tearful** (John 11:35, 43).

Pain

Jesus suffered terrible **pain** when he was flogged (Mark 15:15). He also felt **suffering** (Luke 24:26; Heb. 2:18; 1 Pet. 2:21), **hungry** (Matt. 4:2; 21:18), **thirsty** (John 19:28), and **weary** (John 4:6).

Surprise

Jesus felt **amazed** by the faith of the Roman officer (Luke 7:9). He also felt **astonished** as he prayed to his Abba about his cross (Mark 14:33).

Hope

Jesus' love for God and us comes from his **hope** (1 Cor. 13:7; Col. 1:5). He also felt **curious** (Luke 19:5).

Trust

Jesus lived by **faith** (confident trust) in God, showing us how to do it. In Galatians 2:20 Paul says, "I live by the faith of the Son of God" (KJV). (See also 2:16; 3:22.)

Love

Jesus felt genuine **love** for people like the rich young ruler (Mark 10:21); Martha, Mary, and Lazarus (John 11:5); and his disciples as he washed their feet (John 13:1). He also felt **friendship love** (John 11:3; 20:2), **compassion** (Matt. 9:36; 14:14; 15:32; 20:34), and **empathy** (Heb. 4:15).

Joy

Jesus was exceedingly **joyful** when he saw that seventy-two ordinary disciples were able to minister the power of God's kingdom to people (Luke 10:21). He also felt **rejoicing** (John 11:15), **gladness** (John 15:11; 17:13), and **thankfulness** (Matt. 11:25).

Peace

Jesus felt **peace** from heaven's world and shared this with his disciples before he died (John 14:27). He also felt **rest** (Matt. 11:28) and **refreshment** (Mark 6:31).

SOUL TALK

1. What do you think about the idea that we can be emotionally lost?
2. What did you learn about how empathy fosters secure attachment?
3. What was your experience with reading Jesus' "Tender Beatitudes"?
4. How does it feel to imagine Jesus as your Good Shepherd looking for you when you feel lost?
5. Which of Jesus' thirty-nine emotions do you especially relate to?

3

Self-Empathy Relies on Grace

Love others as much as you love yourself.

Mark 12:31 CEV

I (Bill) think everyone I've talked with over the years struggles with self-judging to some extent. This undermines our spiritual growth and joy in life. When we lack empathy for our emotions and needs, our inner attitude or self-talk may sound like this: "You shouldn't feel this . . . You're burdening people with your needs . . . Don't be a complainer . . . Don't cry . . . You'll get hurt . . . Stay in control . . ." Even as we share personally with a friend or cry out to God in prayer, this inner judge may try to shame us.

When you feel ambushed by judgments like these, stop and think about this: *Jesus had emotional needs and asked for empathy*. The eternal and almighty Son of God humbled himself to become a human being who needed empathy. As a child, Jesus received empathy from others, especially his mother, who treasured all his words in her heart, and this helped him to grow in his experience of God's favor (Luke 2:51–52). As an adult our Lord asked for empathy from his Father and also from people. Here are a few examples:

Jesus asked the Samaritan woman at the well, "Please give me a drink" (John 4:7 NLT).

He arranged with Simon to relax in his house on the Sabbath (Mark 1:29).

To limit the crowds and commotion, Jesus often asked people not to tell anyone that he had healed them (e.g., Matt. 8:4).

He wanted to spend some quiet days as a guest in Martha's house (Luke 10:38).

He prayed, "Please give to us the food that we need each day" (Luke 11:3 EASY).

He asked the owner of a house, "Please show us the room where [we] may eat the Passover meal" (Luke 22:11 ICB).

Jesus was very vulnerable with Peter, James, and John when he shared, "My heart is very sad. I am almost dying! Stay here and watch with me" (Matt. 26:38 WE).

He pleaded in prayer, "Abba . . . take this cup from me" (Mark 14:36).

On the cross he cried, "I am thirsty" (John 19:28).

Jesus cried out in pain and wept in sorrow, and God answered him (Heb. 5:7).

If Jesus, the Son of God who had perfect faith, needed empathy, how much more do we need it! That's why he repeatedly taught us to ask for what we need (e.g., Matt. 7:7–8; John 14:14; 16:24) and be empathetic with one another. "In everything, do to others what you would have them do to you" (Matt. 7:12).

> *Dear Jesus, help us take courage to be vulnerable, ask for the empathy we need, and dare to agree with your grace always. Fill us up with your words of empathy, forgiveness, and truth so that we would be strengthened to love others as you do.*

Missing the Empathy You Need

The prophet Jeremiah pointed out, "You can't heal a wound by saying it's not there" (Jer. 6:14 TLB). It's obvious if you think about it, but that's not what I (Bill) was taught on the football field. We were all about denying wounds, pushing through pain, and continually fighting to win, no matter how tired we felt. That was my philosophy for life too. It seemed to protect me from feeling hurt and gave me courage to push through difficulties. Whatever situation I was in, I denied my feelings and pushed to get the ball across the goal line. If I didn't make it, I got frustrated at myself and tried harder next time.

Sometimes my football mentality returns. Like the time I burned my finger pulling soup out of the microwave. I yelled out in pain and rubbed my blistered finger. Kristi tried to comfort me with words of empathy and offered to put a soothing gel on the burn, but I put up a wall by saying, "I should've been more careful. It's nothing. Let's eat." Then we prayed and started eating. I was mad at myself for being careless and I sulked in self-pity and got grumpy. That's what happens when you spoil empathy and grace. But after a while, I came back to my senses and received Kristi's comfort. Burning my finger is a little thing, but *denying love is a big thing.* If I was missing empathy in small difficulties, how much more was I missing empathy in the bigger difficulties that come my way?

At times we all miss God's empathy because of unconscious inner resistances to feeling pain and being vulnerable. The Enneagram is the best spiritual psychology tool we've found to help us identify and overcome resistances that sabotage personal growth. We go deep into this in our book *Healthy Feelings, Thriving Faith*. For now, it'll help you to understand that each personality type has a core wound (or root sin) that it keeps denying rather than trusting Jesus' empathy, which helps us to receive God's forgiveness, grace, and wisdom. Here is a brief summary of how each of us can get stuck in the unhealthy resistance of our type and miss the empathy of Jesus that we need.

How Enneagram Types Miss Empathy

Ones feel inadequate and seek improvement, not empathy.

Twos feel unwanted and seek appreciation, not empathy.

Threes feel unsuccessful and seek achievement, not empathy.

Fours feel ordinary and seek specialness, not empathy.

Fives feel alone and seek more knowledge, not empathy.

Sixes feel fear and seek safe situations, not empathy.

Sevens feel bored and seek pleasure, not empathy.

Eights feel weak and seek power, not empathy.

Nines feel lethargic and seek merger with others, not empathy.

Understanding Self-Empathy

I (Kristi) had a favorite cat named Charlie. He delighted in my affection and had a special bond with me. Often, he would sit in my lap, knead on my tummy with his paws, and purr—like he did with his mommy when he was a kitty. He was self-soothing. He had internalized the comfort of nursing and was replicating this. Often children do the same thing with their mother, father, or another caregiver. Probably they don't knead on someone's tummy! But they use a pacifier, blanket, the name "Mommy," or a picture to help them reconnect with maternal comfort and security. They're developing self-empathy. Adults need self-empathy too; it's how we overcome self-judging and other resistances to needing grace. Self-empathy strengthens you to be able to give empathy and love to other people.

You may not have heard the term "self-empathy." Let's unpack a working definition of giving empathy to yourself:

Self-empathy is agreeing with empathy from God or a loved one to appreciate that you are deeply loved by God.

Self-empathy relies on God's loving, empathetic presence and words to relate to yourself with empathy. Practically speaking, often this looks like trusting a friend to listen to you with empathy and you choosing to believe and appreciate that God is caring for you through your friend. You're looking at yourself through the eyes of the Lord and your friend.

Self-empathy is the opposite of self-rejection and self-criticism. When you dislike yourself, it screens out the love that God and others offer you and makes it hard for your soul to breathe. In times of emotional distress or need, self-empathy is like an oxygen mask. If you're in a plane with your child and the cabin pressure drops, you need to put your oxygen mask on first so you can safely help your child put on their oxygen mask. If you don't care for yourself then you can't very well care for others.

One time when David and his men returned to their camp at Ziklag, they found it destroyed by fire and their wives and children taken captive by enemies. They wept uncontrollably till they had no strength left. As the leader, David was in despair, "but David encouraged himself in the LORD his God" (1 Sam. 30:6 KJV). He trusted the Lord for the comfort and strength he needed, and then he was able to rise up and lead his men to rescue their families. That's self-empathy. David, in his psalms of lament, shows us how to use self-empathy to agree with God's grace.

Henri Nouwen, author of many books on Christian spirituality, taught that the way to overcome distressed emotions is not to fight against them, deny them, or judge them as weak and problematic, but to *befriend our emotions*.[1] To be friendly to your emotions is to be patient, gentle, and accepting of them. It's to listen to your emotions and learn from them (without being controlled by them).

Let's be clear that *self-empathy is not a do-it-yourself project*; it's not helping yourself in an independent and self-sufficient way apart from God. After all, "self-help is no help at all" (Luke 9:24 MSG). When you place your troubled heart in the strong and empathetic hands of God, he lifts you up, cares deeply for you, and warms you up so you can shine with the glorious light of Christ (1 Pet. 5:6–7; Matt. 5:16).

Self-empathy is relying on the empathy of Jesus, who calls you his friend (John 15:15). The Lord "consoles us as we endure the pain and hardship of life so that we may draw from His comfort and share it with others in their own struggles" (2 Cor. 1:4 VOICE). To develop self-empathy and give empathy to others, you need to believe that God, who is the source of perfect love, sees you and cares for you. Self-empathy puts faith in the Lord's grace and understanding for our weaknesses, shortcomings, emotions, and needs. Then we can overflow with empathy for others.

To receive any aspect of God's grace, like empathy, it's important to feel your need for it and accept it with gratitude. In other words, you are agreeing with God's grace. That's what Jesus did in the Scriptures quoted at the beginning of this chapter. Self-empathy implicitly says, *I need this and that's okay.* You're exercising self-empathy when you:

- Pray with emotional honesty (Ps. 56)
- Identify with the suffering of others (1 Pet. 5:9)
- Ask for what you need (Matt. 7:7, 11)
- Trust that God is gracious and helpful with your weaknesses (Rom. 8:26)
- Give thanks for God's many blessings to you (Eph. 1:3)

In each of those examples of self-empathy there is a part of you that is understanding, valuing, and caring for your felt needs as you trust your heavenly Father, the source of "every good and perfect gift" (James 1:17).

Self-Empathy Is Not Self-Pity

When Bill and I (Kristi) speak on the importance of self-empathy, occasionally someone objects, "But isn't self-empathy the same as self-pity? I don't want to feel sorry for myself and wallow in the mire of my selfish emotions." Actually, *true self-empathy is the opposite of self-pity.* To engage in self-pity is to sulk in excessive unhappiness about your troubles and try to suck other people into your melancholy swirl (like Bill did after he burned his finger). In contrast, self-empathy seeks to understand your emotions and needs in order to learn how to more fully love God, yourself, and others. Self-pity says, "Poor me!" Self-empathy says, "Let's agree with God's grace."

Self-pity is not truly consoling, and it certainly does not help us deal with our problems. We get stuck on our pity pot, whining about what's wrong in our life and soliciting others to buy into our negativity. In the table below we spell out the contrasting attitudes and behaviors of self-pity and self-empathy.

Self-Pity vs. Self-Empathy

SELF-PITY	SELF-EMPATHY
Doing what you want without regard for others	Considering your needs and others' needs
Not taking responsibility for your life	Accepting responsibility for your life
Indulging your emotions and desires	Engaging in mutually beneficial relationships
Being absorbed with your emotions without thinking	Feeling your emotions and thinking about them
Having a victim mentality and seeking to be rescued	Caring for yourself in order to be more loving
Complaining about your external problems	Understanding your emotions and needs
Being stuck in a melancholy mood	Finding hope for a positive step to take
Bent on escaping hard times	Ready to learn from hard times
Not trusting that God is loving you in your difficulties	Trusting God to work good in what feels bad

The Psychology of Self-Empathy

The Lord Jesus baked the psychology of self-empathy into his great commandment to love God "with all your heart, soul, mind, and strength" and "love others *as much as you love yourself*" (Mark 12:30–31 CEV, emphasis added). Understanding your emotions and caring for your needs through self-empathy is an important part of loving yourself as God loves you. If you don't love yourself as God loves you, then it will hamper your ability to love God and other people and you'll be likely to hit a wall of empathy fatigue (which we discuss in chapter 10).

To care for yourself and others with empathy requires self-differentiation, which is the capacity to differentiate yourself from others in the context of your relationships. Healthy self-differentiation is having good personal boundaries. Psychologically, your "self" refers to your personal identity and includes owning aspects of yourself like your emotions, needs, weaknesses, struggles, sins, strengths, memories, beliefs, values, limits, and choices. If your sense of self is weak, then you will tend to enmesh with others and get emotionally dysregulated. If you have a solid self with healthy self-differentiation, then when you are with other people you are able to feel, accept, and express your unique self and care for the other people at the same time. When you can set boundaries then you can give empathy to others without losing your sense of self.

There have been a number of psychological studies done that show the benefits of self-compassion. Recall our earlier discussion that empathy and compassion are joined at the hip—you can't do one well without the other. The same is true with self-empathy and self-compassion. When you develop self-empathy in dependence upon God's grace, a treasure trove of blessings awaits you!

Benefits of Self-Compassion

- Decreased depression and anxiety[2]
- Increased motivation, healthy behavior, and resilient coping[3]
- Happiness, optimism, and life satisfaction[4]
- Forgiveness and altruism[5]
- Relational connection in romantic relationships[6]

All of us in our spiritual formation process as children learned self-empathy or self-rejection from our parents and other caregivers. Probably we learned both types of self-to-self relating. For instance, if your parent was alcoholic, critical, anxious, depressed, stuck in their head, physically absent, emotionally reactive, emotionally needy, or emotionally detached, then you probably did not receive sufficient empathy as a child. (They may have loved you well in other ways.) You also might be impaired in your ability to receive empathy because of going through trauma or developing unhealthy habits. If you are lacking in self-empathy for any reason, the good news is that you can learn to rely on the grace of Jesus' continual empathy for you.

Relying on Abundant Grace

I (Bill) relate to Paul in the Bible. He seems to be type A and a thinker like me. His story in 2 Corinthians 12 about his thorn in the flesh has had a big impact on me. People debate what this "thorn" was, but the context suggests to me that it was his struggle with being criticized by others (and probably himself). It seems he felt this opposition was slowing him down and inhibiting his success. He prayed to be delivered, but the Lord replied, "My grace is sufficient for you, for my power is made perfect in weakness" (v. 9). *Power in weakness?* That seems like a contradiction. But Paul trusted God's word and received strength and vigor from it. He shows us how to access the power of God's grace in his response of faith: "Therefore I will boast all the more gladly about my weaknesses, so that Christ's power may rest on me. That is why, for Christ's sake, I delight in weaknesses, in insults, in hardships, in persecutions, in difficulties. For when I am weak, then I am strong" (vv. 9–10).

Paul learned to *delight* in his weaknesses. Previously, as a Pharisee he had relied on legalism, self-righteousness, ambition, and anger. But after he met Christ risen from the dead and became his disciple, he learned to rely on God's abundant grace for his weak points and soft spots. He internalized God's tender empathy for his needs, and this gentled his hard-driving and harsh personality. The empathy he received from God he shared with people. For instance, Paul showed empathy for new believers who were burdened by a highly sensitive conscience: "I try my best to be considerate of everyone's feelings" (1 Cor. 10:33 MSG). He joined with the Spirit of God who patiently accepts our weak emotions and needs as opportunities to give us more grace (Rom. 8:26). This helps us to let go of self-judging and learn self-empathy, guided by the wisdom of Scripture. Then we are in position to share God's grace and empathy with others.

One day Charles Spurgeon, the great English preacher of the nineteenth century, was riding his horse home after a hard day's work. He was worn out and deeply discouraged. Suddenly, God's word came to him like a lightning bolt: "My grace is sufficient for *you*." When he realized the divine bounty was for him *personally*, he burst out laughing! Spurgeon imagined himself like a thirsty fish worried to drink the river dry, yet Father River happily tells him to drink freely and assures him, "My stream is sufficient for you!" Then he imagined himself like a little mouse in ancient Egypt, anxious about starving after the seven years of abundance ended, yet Joseph chuckles, "My granaries are sufficient for you!" Finally, he imagined himself as a man standing on a mountain peak, afraid to deplete all the oxygen in the atmosphere, yet the earth chortles, "My atmosphere is sufficient for you!"[7] That's the power of self-empathy—you're joining with and appreciating the abundant sufficiency of God's grace.

Replacing Self-Rejection with Self-Empathy

When I (Kristi) was a girl, it seemed that my parents shielded themselves from my emotions, as if my emotions would hurt them or stress them. Instead of being patient, inquisitive, understanding, and kind toward my emotions, they stayed in their heads, gave me advice, or isolated from me when I had emotions. They thought they were helping me, but I felt rejected. I internalized their attitudes and treated my emotions in the same ways they had done. I judged myself as too sensitive and too emotional, felt shame for my emotions and needs, and hid my heart. I lived with self-rejection.

When I was earning my doctorate in psychology, I started learning how to replace self-rejection with self-empathy by asking for empathy from God and others and carrying it forward by remembering and appreciating it. Then I found that I was much more effective in offering empathy and compassion for others, including my family and friends. Most people welcomed this, but it seemed hard for my mother—it felt to me like she would push away and spoil my empathy. She would even unintentionally shame me for giving it. In her personality she tried to be independent and in control all the time. Probably she had her own unconscious shame for needing empathy and feared being disappointed. After attending our Soul Shepherding Institute retreats, she learned about the importance of empathy, apologized for not giving me empathy as a child, and humbled herself to receive empathy from me. It was a great gift for me to be able to love her in that way. Then I received an additional surprising gift when *she* learned to give empathy to *me*!

Even with all the healing and growth I've experienced, sometimes when I'm carrying a lot of emotions, I step into a shame sinkhole and find myself hiding my emotions and isolating in self-pity. In those situations self-rejection overcomes me, though I may not be able to identify that until I'm out of the sinkhole. It has helped me when Bill or a friend notices that I am not myself and offers me empathy. For instance, one time recently Bill drew me out and listened with a soft heart. After a while he commented, "It seems you might be feeling shame." I was not even aware that I felt shame. All I knew was that I was in pain and didn't want to be. But at that moment my soul woke up as I realized, "He sees me. He cares and he's being gentle with me." That gave me courage to come out of hiding, trust him with my deeper emotions, and agree with his empathy.

In my emotional battle it was God's empathy, Bill's empathy, and my self-empathy that pulled me out of the shame sinkhole. Receiving three-way empathy (which we introduced in chapter 2) empowers you to overcome being stuck in a problem or having your personal growth sabotaged by shame or another unhealthy pattern. We express this in our adage that we teach to our students and clients: *You'll get help when you and I join God in caring for you.*

There are four steps to using three-way empathy to join with God's care and overcome self-rejection:

How to Replace Self-Rejection with Self-Empathy

1. Look to God as your source of perfect love, including empathy.
2. Share your emotions with an ambassador of Jesus' empathy (2 Cor. 5:20).
3. Recognize and resist your internal judge that shames you.
4. Internalize and agree with the empathy you receive (using self-empathy).

We can diagram the development of self-empathy like this:

Trust God → Receive friend's empathy →
Resist judgment → Employ self-empathy

In actual experience, overcoming self-judgment and self-rejection is messier than that. Receiving empathy is not linear—we go back and forth between the four steps. Furthermore, at the same time we are learning self-empathy, our family and friends are needing empathy from us. Inevitably, we step on each other's toes and each of us needs to take a turn setting aside our own felt needs for the moment in order to empathize with the other.

Feeling Reflections for Self-Empathy

Attuning to your emotions (the second of the Four A's of Empathy) with feeling reflection statements that express Jesus' empathy for you can help you overcome your self-judgment and self-rejection (see appendix 2 for a list of empathy statements).

By appreciating and agreeing with Jesus' empathy you're using self-empathy.

Below we articulate one feeling reflection for each Enneagram type to help you overcome your core wound as described earlier in this chapter. You'll probably especially relate to the one for your personality type and perhaps to one from your wing (one of the numbers to either side of yours). You may want to underline the statement that helps you and keep repeating it to yourself till it becomes a natural part of your prayers, self-talk, and requests for empathy from a friend.

Feeling Reflection Statements

One: "You're trying so hard to reach your ideals and it's frustrating to be thwarted."

Two: "It seems you feel insecure and bad about yourself unless you're appreciated."

Three: "Underneath your achievements it seems you feel inadequate."

Four: "It seems when you see your colleagues' success it makes you feel inferior."

Five: "Maybe you're afraid that person will overwhelm you and exhaust you."

Six: "It's difficult for you to quiet your mind, stop worrying, and feel your emotions."

Seven: "It seems you felt bored and antsy at that meeting—it was hard for you to focus."

Eight: "Injustice makes you angry, especially when it affects someone you care for."

Nine: "It seems that disagreement made you feel upset and anxious."

If you're not familiar with the Enneagram or want to receive more empathy for the needs and emotions of your personality type, you'll appreciate our book *Healthy Feelings, Thriving Faith*, which includes sections on Jesus' empathy for each type and seven empathy statements for each type.[8]

EMPATHY PRACTICE:

Empathy Prayer

Empathy Prayer is a template for writing an emotionally honest letter to Jesus and receiving an empathetic letter back from him.[9] It's similar to some of the psalms of lament (e.g., Ps. 3). In our Institute retreats people say this is one of their favorite spiritual practices that we teach. First, they write their letters in private prayer. Later, they take turns reading them out loud with a partner to give empathy to one another.

There are four steps in our practice of Empathy Prayer:

1. Talk to Jesus, addressing him personally and thanking him for his care.
2. Identify a particular situation in your life today in which you need his empathy.
3. Listen for Jesus' empathy about your physical demeanor, thoughts, emotions, and the magnitude of those emotions.
4. Listen for an affirmation and encouraging Scripture from the Lord.

To exchange letters with Jesus, simply follow the prompts below.

Your Letter to Jesus

Dear Jesus, my ________________ *(identify a favorite name for Jesus, like Shepherd or Lord) . . .*

I appreciate how you have cared for me (share a memory of experiencing God's blessing) . . .

Today, I need your help with (briefly describe a specific situation of need) . . .

Jesus' Letter to You

Dear _____________________ *(your name),*

I see your physical demeanor of (e.g., rushing around, carrying heavy responsibilities, tossing and turning in bed, clenching your jaw, slumping your shoulders, frowning, crying) . . .

I hear what you are saying (or thinking in your mind) . . .

I understand you are feeling (e.g., anxiety, shame, anger, sadness, or other emotions) . . .

I know this is really big for you because you need . . .

I enjoy being with you and affirm you as a person who is (e.g., emotionally honest, trusting, courageous, kind, persevering, faithful) . . .

I want to encourage you by sharing a Scripture (e.g., a Bible promise) . . .

SOUL TALK

1. What do you think about the teaching that denying emotions spoils God's empathy?
2. What did you learn about developing self-empathy to agree with God's grace?
3. What helps you to trust that God's grace is abundantly sufficient for you?
4. Which feeling reflection statement did you relate to most? What's an example of a situation where you need that empathy?
5. What was your experience with using the Empathy Prayer template to exchange letters with Jesus? If you shared this experience with a friend, how did that feel?

Empathy Loves Others

I have you in my heart . . . you share in God's grace with me.

Philippians 1:7

The Spirit of Jesus speaks to you through Paul's words above. Jesus has you in his heart. He feels for you and extends God's grace to you. This letter that Paul wrote from prison exudes the joy he feels in knowing Jesus intimately and sharing his grace with other people. He invites us to join him and share with one another a windfall of blessings from Christ: encouragement, comfort, common sharing, tenderness, compassion, being like-minded, love, having one spirit and one mind, humility, valuing others above self, and supporting the interests of others (Phil. 2:1–4).

Did you notice that Paul uses a string of *empathy words*? Reread the sentence above and appreciate the empathy that's embedded there. Even as Bible students we may miss this.

The point is that empathy helps us develop "the same mindset as Christ Jesus" (Phil. 2:5). It's easy to take empathy for granted, yet it's essential to giving and receiving love in all of our relationships.

Paul teaches that the Son of God set aside the advantages of being in the Trinity in heaven, came to earth, and "made himself nothing by taking the very nature of a servant, being made in human likeness . . . becoming obedient to death—even death on a cross" (Phil. 2:6–8). That's perfect empathy that blossoms into total forgiveness and unfailing love.

Thank you, Lord Jesus, for leaving heaven to become like us so we can become like you. It's our honor and joy to share with others your humble and empathetic love.

Screaming on the Inside

One evening at a Soul Shepherding Institute retreat, I (Bill) opened with a Scripture meditation on Jesus' transfiguration and guided everyone to repeat a quiet Breath Prayer, "Jesus, be the center" (based on Matt. 21:9 NLT).[1] Then I invited everyone to partner up and listen to each other with empathy as they shared their Journey Maps of how they've experienced God (or not) in the ups and downs of life.[2] I noticed that Heather did not find a partner and had walked off by herself, so I went to her and asked if she wanted me to listen and pray for her.

After we sat down, Heather pulled out her map with trembling hands and described an event that happened when she was an eight-year-old girl. She had been playing with her older brother in the woods behind their house when suddenly her dad ran out, yanked her brother away by the arm, began yelling at him, and gave him a whooping. Heather watched in horror as her brother cried out in pain, sobbed, and collapsed limp on the ground. She was petrified and mute. She blamed herself: "Why didn't I scream? Mom would've run outside and stopped the beating. I'm such a wuss!"

I consoled her with empathy, "It was frightening to see your dad abuse your brother." Tearing up, she shared more. Then I noticed that she was slumping in her chair, so I reflected back to her, "It seems that, like your brother, you've collapsed limp, paralyzed with shame. You also absorbed your dad's rage and abuse. It wasn't safe for you to get angry at your father so you've been whipping yourself with anger and feeling bad about yourself for not being stronger to protect your brother. The truth is that you were a little girl and just as vulnerable and in need of protection as your brother. You both were abused that day."

When she was done sharing, I asked her if she wanted to find her voice by taking the hand of Jesus, going into the woods, and screaming for help. Suddenly, Heather's eyes got as big as saucers and she exclaimed, "At the start of our group session tonight when you had us pray 'Jesus, be the center,' I sensed the Holy Spirit ask me to put my hand on my heart. As I did that, in my mind I heard the words 'Go into the woods and scream—I will stand with you.' I felt a wave of warm love come over me, but I still didn't trust that I was really hearing God. But your suggestion confirms this for me."

I asked if she'd like to receive emotionally healing prayer. I explained that even though this would not change the history of the abuse incident, God could heal the effects it was having on her. God could help her to feel her anger, give voice to it, and heal the shame and fear that were continuing to hurt her and hold her back. She said she did want to engage in healing prayer, so I guided her to visit the abuse memory in quiet prayer and ask Jesus to spiritually go into the woods with her. I invited her adult self to take the hand of the Lord Jesus and walk into this memory in prayer to care for the little girl in her history and heart. Through her experience of healing prayer, she received empathy directly from the Spirit of Jesus. Being understood and bonded with her Lord gave her comfort and strength. As she held Jesus' hand, he stood beside her and she screamed for help. She found her voice and verbalized her anger at her father. Then she cried as Jesus embraced little Heather and her brother. The power of Jesus' empathy took away her shame and fear.

Previously, Heather had unconsciously converted her anger at her father into shame, blaming herself for not stopping the abuse. Her shame had been keeping the love of God at bay so it couldn't reach her inner child. But now she had a corrective emotional experience. How did I support this? Mostly, I simply gave her empathy and prayed for her. Afterwards, I validated the significance of her healing prayer experience, suggesting that it was a breakthrough to keep thanking God for. I affirmed her bravery to revisit this memory with me, feel the painful emotions, and put her trust in the Lord Jesus. Later she did more inner work on her relationship with her dad to pray for him, develop Jesus' heart of empathy for his pain, and forgive him.[3]

Empathy Takes Away Shame

I (Kristi) have noticed countless times that when a person has an emotional response that no one else seems to have, they feel shame. As you saw in Heather's story, shame is a stubborn resistance to God's grace that can get a choke hold on a person for years, even a whole lifetime. It suffocates our souls *anytime we are hurting and feel rejected or alone.* This can happen in subtle, hidden ways.

When Bill and I launched our book *Journey of the Soul* into the public, it was an exciting culmination of many years of learning and ministry. But it also felt very vulnerable, and I was scared to be going way out on a limb. I had risked sharing some of my deepest hurts, best insights, and untold hours of work. How would readers respond? Would church leaders and event planners still want us to speak? I was caught in a whirlwind of upsetting emotions. Then shame started strangling me: *I'm too emotional and insecure. I shouldn't be so afraid—I don't have enough faith . . . Worse, I'm being proud and wanting success.*

But Bill listened to me and was gentle with my emotions. He also shared his own fears about how our book would be received and was vulnerable with me about his struggles with judging himself. I wasn't alone. *Empathy lifted me out of shame and helped me accept my emotions.* I joined with Bill's empathy to have empathy for myself, and most of all I trusted God. "Those who look to [the Lord] for help will be radiant with joy; no shadow of shame will darken their faces" (Ps. 34:5 NLT).

Recently I was having lunch with a friend and she was sharing a big challenge she's having with her son. She was afraid she was burdening me and was falling into shame. When I told her I was truly happy to listen to her with empathy and pray for her, it melted away her icy shame.

Loving One Another

Everybody needs empathy to know they are deeply loved and to flourish in their life. As followers of Jesus, we are called to give empathetic care to the poor, marginalized people, enemies, and strangers. Yet, the Bible puts first priority on our giving and receiving empathetic care with our family and friends. This is the meaning of Jesus' commandments to "love your neighbor" and "love one another." These close relationships make up our school of discipleship for becoming more like Jesus, and they prepare us for reaching out with empathy to love other people who live farther away or are not part of our daily life.

"Love one another"[4] was a recurring message of Jesus, repeated fifteen times in the New Testament by Jesus himself or his apostles. All told, there are fifty-eight specific times we are taught to empathetically care for "one another" (or "each other") in the New Testament.[5] These represent a cornucopia of practical ways to offer empathy and compassion to bless others, especially those who are near and dear. Here are some highlights:

Empathetic "One Another" Scriptures

"Love each other like brothers and sisters" (Rom. 12:10 NCV).

"Live in harmony with one another" (Rom. 12:16).

"Stop passing judgment on one another" (Rom. 14:13).

"Accept one another" (Rom. 15:7).

"Serve one another humbly in love" (Gal. 5:13).

"Be kind and compassionate to one another" (Eph. 4:32).

"Bear with each other" (Col. 3:13).

"Encourage one another" (1 Thess. 5:11).

"Pray for each other" (James 5:16).

"Love one another deeply, from the heart" (1 Pet. 1:22).

"Echo God's intense love for one another" (1 Pet. 4:8 TPT).

"Offer hospitality to one another" (1 Pet. 4:9).

You've probably noticed many of these "one another" instructions in the Bible, but maybe you have not realized they are *expressions of empathy*. You need empathy from other people, and they need it from you. Reread the list of "one another" instructions above in view of what you've been learning about empathy, and we think you'll agree that they speak to the importance of empathy in our families, friendships, church communities, neighborhoods, and workplace relationships.

The PACE of Empathy

When Jesus sent his disciples out for ministry into the surrounding villages, he instructed them not to carry extra supplies or worry about what to say or do, but to trust God to love people through them. He told them, "You don't need a lot of equipment. *You* are the equipment" (Matt. 10:10 MSG). This is true in the ministry of empathy. What is most helpful to people is not your skills or knowledge but *your heart.* The more empathy lives *in you* the more it can flow *out of you.* To paraphrase the beloved disciple, *Beloved, let us empathize with one another, for empathy comes from God* (1 John 4:7).[6] An important way that we give and receive God's empathetic love is with people in the body of Christ (1 Cor. 12:27–28), ministering Christ's friendship to one another (2 Cor. 5:20 MSG).

I (Bill) have learned over the years that in order to listen with empathy and appreciate it from others, we need to slow our pace. Even if we're sitting in a chair, our mind may flit about with distractions. As with listening to God in Scripture, listening to people is supported by breathing deeply, centering ourselves in God, and being emotionally present. "Love is patient" (1 Cor. 13:4). *It is unhurried.* It's like Jacob in the Bible slowing down to go at the pace of the children and animals (Gen. 33:14). Being unhurried supports heartfelt and thoughtful listening to God and people.

Much to our surprise, Kristi and I have learned a great deal about empathy from speaking to groups of Spanish-speaking people and being translated. When a speaker is partnered with an expert translator, typically it moves very fast and they talk over each other. This is very efficient for disseminating as much content as possible in the allotted time. But Kristi and I have taken the approach of cutting our content in half and not talking fast. This gives more breathing space for listeners to absorb what we're teaching (in both languages) and to reflect on their own thoughts and feelings about what they're learning. It's especially true in a personal conversation that when you slow down your pace to listen carefully and allow silent pauses for each of you to feel, think, relate, and reflect together, it facilitates the power of empathy to provide cathartic release, comfort, insight, and appreciation of what the Spirit of Jesus is saying and doing in the moment.

We use PACE as an acrostic to teach four related types of empathy: *prayerful* empathy, *affective* empathy, *cognitive* empathy, and *effective* empathy. When you're listening to someone share personally, especially if you're shepherding them, it's ideal if you have opportunity to give all four types of empathy, but even if you can give only one or two, that is still caring and helpful. Let's consider each one.

Prayerful Empathy

The most important expression of empathy is prayer. Throughout my life I (Kristi) was blessed because my mom met weekly with her friend to pray. One day when I was sixteen, my mom's prayer partner, Jan, came to our house and asked me how I was doing. I told her that we had been shopping for a car for me to drive to school and church and had narrowed it down to two choices: a brown Honda Civic or a blue Volkswagen Rabbit with a sunroof. I didn't tell her that I wanted the fun blue VW, because I knew my parents wanted me to get the practical brown Civic. Later, when my mom and Jan were praying, I was surprised to overhear Jan say with empathy, "Lord, Kristi really wants the blue car. Please guide Betty and Kristi in this decision." I was so touched that she perceived my heart's secret desire and prayed earnestly for our decision. Sure enough, God answered Jan's prayer and I got the blue VW!

For my whole life, my mom's prayers for my family and me have been an enormous gift. I wanted to pass on this legacy to our children and grandchildren, so I started a Moms in Prayer group when our first child started kindergarten, and I have continued in a group to this day. Over the years, it's been such a blessing to gather with friends and listen to each other's prayers. I feel incredible empathy and love when a friend prays for my requests because I hear that she has understood my heart and has joined in with me to cry out to the Lord for my child's need.

Not only are the best prayers empathetic, it's also true that the best empathy is prayerful. Prayer, whether spoken or silent, solitary or social, builds a spiritual bridge between God and people. Secret intercessions are a special way to serve and help others. You can do this while you're listening to someone share. As you listen, you trust God to be their helper and shoot up little prayers now and again like, "Jesus, she's feeling sad . . . Care for my friend . . . Father, we need your wisdom . . . Holy Spirit, you are here—what do you want to say or do? . . . Thank you, Lord, for loving my friend . . ." When you pray with love for people and have faith in God, you will eventually see evidence of God acting, often in ways that surprise you.

Affective Empathy

You've probably heard the saying "Love is not a feeling." It's true, love is a *choice* and it's important to be able to love someone even when you don't feel like it. But that dictum is not *all* true because *normally love includes emotion.* If your spouse or best friend "loved" you but never or rarely had any emotional expression in their love for you, then probably you would not believe you were deeply loved by them. Love that stays detached from emotion is a duty that needs to be warmed up.

It's important that the love we give and receive is tender-hearted, compassionate, and comes with a smile. You feel deeply loved when someone *genuinely enjoys loving you*. As you've seen in the empathy Scriptures we've been referring to, the Bible repeatedly calls us to develop empathetic love for one another (see appendix 1 for more empathy Scriptures).

The heart of empathy is called affective empathy because we are recognizing and resonating with one another's emotions to feel what they feel and express care. It's less about the words we say and more about *the way* we show warmth, curiosity, goodwill, or concern in our faces, eyes, posture, hands, and tone of voice. It's being *emotionally touched* by one another's hurts, burdens, and needs. Affective empathy seeks to go a little deeper than what was said. It understands the emotions that underlie circumstances and thoughts.

Affective empathy needs careful boundaries. As listeners we need boundaries on our affective empathy so it doesn't decline into enmeshment, coddling, or getting overloaded by other people's emotions. As people who need empathy, it's important to be emotionally honest with safe people, take personal responsibility, and appreciate the grace of empathy that's given.

Whenever I (Kristi) stay at a hotel or Airbnb, I feel affective empathy for the person who cleans our room. While in high school, I volunteered to serve at a conference center one summer. One of my jobs was to clean a section of hotel rooms. Many people left their room looking as if a tornado had gone through it. My memories of how I felt move me to act with empathy by leaving our room in good shape and thanking the housekeeping staff. In that situation affective empathy sounds like, "Thank you for cleaning our room so carefully. I know it's a lot of work and I really appreciate it." Their faces always brighten when I say something like that. Not many people thank them or even smile at them.

Cognitive Empathy

Cognitive empathy focuses on gaining mental clarity on what people are thinking and feeling. *Mental clarity? Isn't empathy about emotions?* Perhaps you're wondering why cognitive or mental empathy is important. Many people don't realize that empathy tunes in to people's thoughts, not just their emotions. Thinking and feeling are connected, even in our brains. Atticus Finch shows cognitive empathy in *To Kill a Mockingbird* when he remarks, "You never really understand a person until you consider things from his point of view—until you climb into his skin and walk around in it."[7]

Bill and I (Kristi) often talk with people who believe they can't be good at empathy because they're head types and struggle to feel emotions. But that's not true. Cognitive empathy is an essential component of empathy, and it comes primarily from thinking. This means that people who are thoughtful and curious can get good at this type of empathy quickly and be a real help to others. With practice, it can even warm you up to express more emotion in your empathy.

When I was younger, I acted in plays and learned how to imagine myself in my character. *What was it like to be her in this situation? What was her facial expression? What was the energy in her body? What was she thinking and saying to herself in her mind? What was she feeling and wanting?* That sort of perspective-taking is cognitive empathy. In a conversation when you're listening to someone this might sound like, "I imagine you're thinking that it's not fair. If I were you I think I'd feel angry."

Effective Empathy

Ashley had been learning about empathy at one of our Institute retreats. One afternoon she was browsing in a boutique (prayerfully with Jesus!) when suddenly a woman burst through the doors, making a distressed commotion. "I need help! I need a dress for my niece's wedding. I forgot to pack one and the wedding starts in ten minutes." Ashley immediately felt for the woman *and* she acted with compassion. She went right up to her and said, "We've got this. What's your dress size? Okay, go in the dressing room and I'll hand you dresses to try on." The woman liked the third dress, and as she ran to the counter, Ashley ripped the tag off and exclaimed, "Go! Go! You look great!" Breathless, the woman opened her purse, but the cashier smiled and said, "It's been paid for!" The woman started crying, "Thank you so much! I was just diagnosed with cancer and haven't been able to think straight." That's empathy blossoming into compassion.

Empathy in action is called effective empathy because it is concerned with understanding people's practical challenges and needs and then supporting them with the next step they can take to move forward. Examples of effective empathy include saying things such as, "It sounds like you've been stuck on this issue for a while and need a fresh idea for how to make progress" and "When you've struggled with this issue in the past, what helped you?"

Giving the Four A's of Empathy to Others

When you reflect on Heather's story from earlier in this chapter, you might think, *I couldn't do that for someone. I'm not a psychologist like Bill. I'm not trained in therapy or healing prayer.* Don't accept those thoughts! The main thing I (Bill) did that was helpful was to give Heather empathy by listening (see appendix 3 for descriptions of six practical skills on how to LISTEN well). Jesus' little brother urged, "Lead with your ears, follow up with your tongue" (James 1:19 MSG). Active listening is like volleying a tennis ball across a net with a friend. Your goal as the listener is to keep hitting the ball back by saying things like, "What happened to stress you? . . . It seems you feel . . . This was really big for you because . . . I admire your heart of . . ."

In my volleys back to Heather, I used the Four A's of Empathy: asking her questions, attuning to her emotions, acknowledging the significance of her experience, and affirming her strengths (see below). You too can do this for the people you listen to and care for. It may feel awkward or stiff at first. That's normal when learning any new skill. Just stay humble, taking the attitude that you are a student of the person you're caring for. Even when you don't use the "right" words, don't sweat it. If your heart's intention is to understand and care for your friend, that's empathy! It will come through. But even if you're not connecting with people as well as you want to, if you persevere in your own inner journey of receiving empathy from Jesus and others, then this will go a long way to put more empathy inside you so you can naturally overflow with empathy for others (2 Cor. 1:4).

Let me unpack for you how I used the Four A's of Empathy to support Heather's emotional healing and help meet her personal needs to feel seen, understood, accepted, and valued by Jesus.

1. **Ask** QUESTIONS

When I saw that Heather didn't have a partner to share with, I asked if she'd like me to listen to her. During the conversation I asked about her experience and emotions, inviting her to share more. Sometimes I simply said, "Tell me more about that . . ." (I was volleying the tennis ball back to her, inviting her to elaborate.) Later I asked her if she'd like me to pray for her. Asking questions like these may seem like such a little thing, but she would tell you how she felt seen, wanted, and deeply cared for from this approach.

2. **Attune** to emotions

   I opened my heart to what she was feeling. First, I saw that she was alone. When we sat down, I noticed her trembling hands as she held her Journey Map, and I mirrored back that she seemed to feel frightened. After she shared her traumatic story, I saw that she collapsed limp in her chair as her brother had done after the whipping, so I commented that maybe she felt paralyzed with shame. My feeling reflections helped her feel understood and supported. She began to sit up straight and her face brightened. She was able to regulate her emotional distress.

   My attuning empathy for Heather was an expression of Jesus' attuning empathy for her—that's the most important thing. Jesus came into the foreground for her twice. First, when Holy Spirit prompted her to prayerfully put her hand on her heart and she felt a wave of warm love come over her body. Then, during the emotionally healing prayer time, she felt deeply loved and strengthened by Jesus holding her hand, standing with her to help her scream, and holding her and her brother as she cried.

3. **Acknowledge** the significance

   I acknowledged the big impact this trauma had on Heather when I validated the intensity of her emotions, using feeling words like *terrified*, *shame*, *rage*, *abuse*, *vulnerable*, and *in need of protection*. Additionally, I emphasized the significance of her experience that she shared with me when I called it a *breakthrough* to keep thanking God for. I did this because I wanted to help her cherish Jesus' gift of emotional healing so she wouldn't doubt it later. The fact that I experienced her emotions and Jesus' ministry to her helped her to feel validated and accepted.

4. **Affirm** strengths

At the end of Heather's time of sharing and prayer, I affirmed her for being so brave and emotionally honest and for reaching out to the Lord Jesus with faith. Notice that *I saved my encouraging words for the end of the conversation.* (That's why this is the fourth A.) We've observed that if well-meaning helpers offer words of encouragement or affirmation to a hurting or stressed person too soon, it closes their heart and they stop being vulnerable. Instead of feeling understood and cared for by you, they are likely to feel pressured to do better or judged for struggling. By waiting to offer affirmations until after you've asked questions, attuned to their emotions, and acknowledged the significance of their experiences, you're providing the support and time they need to release their distress, feel understood by you, and experience a caring bond with you. Then your affirming words can give them dignity and lift their spirits.

EMPATHY PRACTICE:

Praying for Others with Empathy

Empathy for people's difficulties and needs motivates me (Kristi) to pray for them. But feeling deeply for their situation can also tap my energy and weigh me down. I have learned that when I feel too exhausted or discouraged to pray for others, it's because I'm putting the burden on my little shoulders instead of Jesus' big shoulders. So instead of forcing myself to keep interceding in prayer anyway, I turn my thoughts and feelings to God by renewing my mind in Scripture (Rom. 12:2).

Here are a few Scriptures that can encourage your prayers for others:

> God is a loving Father who has compassion on all his children (Ps. 103:13).
>
> God gave his only Son to us to give us abundant life and defeat Satan (John 3:16; 10:10).
>
> Jesus Christ is the perfect High Priest and he empathizes with our weaknesses (Heb. 4:15).

My risen Lord is right now seated at the right hand of God and interceding for us (Rom. 8:34).

Scriptures like these encourage me that I am not alone. Jesus is with me, ministering God's love. I can join Jesus in his empathy and prayers for others!

These steps can help you pray for your loved one(s) now:

1. Give thanks.
   Lord Jesus, thank you that you are already praying to the Father with empathy and faith for _(name)_.
2. Ask for God's empathy.
   Jesus, please give me God's empathy and knowledge for _(name's)_ *situation and needs.*
3. Quietly listen to the Spirit.
   Holy Spirit, I'm listening for any thoughts or feelings that you impress upon my mind . . .
4. Pray for the loved one's needs.
   Dear Father, with Jesus, I trust you to care for _(name)_ *and her/his struggle with* _________. *I pray that you would provide her/his need for* _________.
5. Rejoice in God's provision.
   Thank you, Lord Jesus, for praying with me and helping me to know God's love, wisdom, power, and grace. I am happy to continue in prayer with you. Amen.

When I join Jesus' empathy and prayers for people, it helps me release the burden of their hurts and problems to God and brings me joy. I pray for you, that you will know the Lord Jesus is delighted you have joined with him in prayer and that you will enjoy Holy Spirit's presence and peace, especially in the matters you have entrusted to God.

SOUL TALK

1. Which are your favorite empathetic "one anothers"? Why?
2. What did you learn about the importance of cognitive empathy and how it's different from and complementary to affective empathy?
3. Which of the four PACE empathy types are you best at: prayerful empathy, affective empathy, cognitive empathy, or effective empathy? How does this feel for you?
4. Which of the Four A's of Empathy do you need to improve on to be more loving?
5. What was your experience with the empathy practice of praying for others?

5

The Grit and Grace of Empathy

We will lovingly follow the truth at all times . . . and so become more and more in every way like Christ.

Ephesians 4:15 TLB

When you give empathy to someone, it's not only gracious, it's also *gritty*. It takes courage to keep opening your heart to their pain. It takes endurance to help carry the weight of their burdens. It takes wisdom to discern when empathy includes speaking a hard truth in love to help them find the strength to act responsibly.

It seems that on almost every page of the Gospels we see Jesus being kind and gracious with all types of people. But when stronger medicine is needed, the Lord Jesus is not Caspar Milquetoast—he challenges and confronts people, as he often did with the Pharisees. His anger was always governed by loving empathy (see chapter 9 for a discussion of anger and empathy). Jesus defended the sexually broken woman from religious abuse and then he gave her the loving challenge "Go now and leave your life of sin" (John 8:11). Often he lovingly prodded his "little faith" disciples to exercise greater faith (Matt. 6:30; 8:26; 14:31; 16:8). He spoke hard truth to the rich young ruler about his greed, and yet what probably was most convicting for the ruler was when "Jesus looked at him and loved him" (Mark 10:21).

Jesus looks at you with tender love. But if you were continuing in sin and refusing his winsome and gentle love, then his love would become more direct and forceful to get your attention. Wouldn't you want that? Wouldn't you rather be challenged or disciplined by the Lord than to continue in a destructive path of sin? It's great help to know the Lord Jesus this way. When we trust that his anger is always governed by love, then we can go so far as to ask him to give us tough love if that's what we need in order to grow.

> *Lord Jesus, you are love. We trust you to speak the truth in love to us to convict us of sin, strengthen our weaknesses, and guide us in your ways.*

Against Empathy?

A leader advised a young pastor, "Avoid empathy. It lets people whine and complain. It fosters selfishness. You want to activate people to take responsibility for their lives and get busy serving God."

A client had barely sat down in my (Bill's) office before he fired off, "I don't need your empathy." He continued, "I don't want you to be like a typical therapist that just listens. Empathy is nice, but it's weak. I'm not touchy-feely—don't coddle me or beat around the bush, just shoot straight. I want your insights and advice so I can get through this hard season and move forward."

You may have encountered people who are against empathy. For instance, recently some Christian authors and influencers have been talking about "toxic empathy" or calling empathy a "sin." What they are really against is not empathy but catering to whatever people want and enabling them to act like victims. They don't understand that *true empathy* is not coddling—it's compassionate and it holds people accountable. It cultivates emotional intelligence, not emotional indulgence. A recent study showed the maturity and power of empathy by finding that employees who received consistent empathy from their manager, compared to those who received little or no empathy, were more productive and innovative and less likely to burn out and leave the company.[1]

Ironically, over the years I've learned that people who say they don't need empathy are usually the ones who need it *the most* but are denying this. Disregarding empathy "protects" them from doing the hard work of learning to feel their emotions, confess their sins and struggles, and soften their heart to give empathy to other people.

"I Don't Want to Coddle My Son"

Hannah plopped down on the chair in my (Kristi's) office and moaned, "I'm exhausted! My son Michael is driving me crazy. He is so needy! We were at the park and he fell down and just sat there crying. I told him that his friend wanted to play with him, but he just cried harder. What's the matter with him that he gets so emotional like this and can't function?"

"It sounds like you're at your wits' end," I reflected. "You really want him to be stronger and more resilient."

She elaborated further, "I kept telling him he was fine and to just get up and he'd feel better. But he just kept crying. Finally, his friend went off to play with some other kids. He's just such a baby!" She paused for a moment, looked at me, and said, "I don't know what to do about it. You know a lot about parenting. What would you do?"

I replied, "I would go to him and say, 'I saw you fall. Did it hurt? Where does it hurt?' Then I would say something like, 'Michael, I imagine you feel embarrassed that you got hurt.' I might add, 'Maybe you're afraid that your friend doesn't want to play with you now?' These are ways I'd give him empathy and try to help him verbalize what he's feeling."

"Oh, I would not do that," Hannah protested. "I don't want to coddle my son. He needs to toughen up. I want him to grow up to be a strong, manly man who can get back up on his feet after getting knocked down."

Hannah didn't realize that giving her son empathy would not be coddling him—it would be caring for him and activating him. As a parent, I found that giving my children empathy helped them to calm down, feel seen and safe, return to a state of joy, and find courage to get back up and deal with their difficult situation. To coddle Michael would be to hover over him in an overprotective way, smother him with sympathy even when he wanted to go back and play with his friend, or not even let him go to the playground again for fear that he'd get hurt.

The real reason Hannah did not give her son empathy was because *she did not value empathy and had not received it herself.* When I gave her empathy, she did not let it touch her heart. Empathy was not inside her, so she did not have it to give to her son or anyone else. I pointed out to her that she was deflecting the empathy that could calm her stress and give her strength. In subsequent conversations she did begin to appreciate the value of empathy. Over time, as she learned to receive empathy, she was able to give it to her son and others.

Shining a Light on False Empathy

Understanding empathy rightly is crucial to knowing that you are deeply loved by God and helping other people to know this. When I (Bill) was a spiritual formation pastor at a megachurch, I saw that there were many people who had a great need for empathy, so over the course of fifteen years I trained one thousand lay counselors in giving empathy to care for the congregation, community, and viewers who watched our televised church service. I have found that many people have misconceptions of empathy that are harmful.

Here are seven examples of the truth that empathy is gritty and gracious. Each one corrects a common misconception of empathy.

1. **Empathy is not coddling.**

   "It seems you are addicted to your feelings," I (Bill) told Roger. "For instance, when you felt upset after having lunch with your mother last week, you got drunk. You had a storm of emotions surging in you and tried to wash them away with wine. That's not helping you. Instead, let's talk about the distress you feel in your relationship with your mother." Roger was coddling himself with wine. His coping mechanism was selfish. He was indulging his desires to drink as a way to numb his emotions of fear, guilt, and anger. Roger's Alcoholics Anonymous (AA) group also spoke the truth in love to him about the harmful effects his drinking was having on him and others. He needed to develop self-control, personal responsibility, and love for others as well as himself.

2. **Empathy is not reassurance.**

   Reassurance is one of the most common empathy mistakes. It's nice and it means well, but it can be hurtful.

Reassurance is like pumping up cheer. It says, "You are going to do a great job on that project—don't worry!" That sort of "look on the bright side" approach shuts down distressed emotions that need care. We all need to have our feelings understood and validated. The only type of reassurance that is helpful is when it's based on facts that you don't know, like if your doctor looks at your CT scan and says, "I have good news. You don't have cancer!"

One year ago, Bill and I (Kristi) had our daughter's three little children overnight. One-year-old Ellie woke up crying in the night. I could see that she was emotionally troubled but not in physical pain or danger. At times like this a parent might say, "You're okay. Go back to sleep" or "There's nothing to be upset about. You're just tired." But placating words like these invalidate emotions and needs. Instead, I comforted her by holding her and saying with a soothing voice, "Gigi is here." But she kept crying in distress. I realized she was whimpering "Ju-Ju," and I remembered that normally she sleeps with her older sister, so I empathized, "You miss Ju-Ju. She's a special sister to you. She's sleeping in the next room, you'll see her in the morning." As soon as she heard me patiently and lovingly put words to her emotions and support her attachment to her older sister, she calmed down and went back to sleep.

3. **Empathy is not tolerance.**

Today it's popular to speak of "my truth" and "your truth," as if what is true depends on a person's perceptions. Being tolerant of people who have different opinions is respectful, but being tolerant of a worldview based on *untruth or deception* is very damaging. When truth is relative to each person it elevates people's subjective emotions, desires, and opinions to a position of authoritative truth (for them personally and anyone they influence). That's not empathy—it's *idolizing emotions*. People who think this way want to be "free" to define reality for themselves rather than submitting to God and the truth he has revealed in his Word and creation. The Lord Jesus taught that *real freedom* comes from understanding and obeying his teachings, which are true and enable us to personally know the truth and live it out in love (John 8:31–32).

John Wesley taught the importance of discerning truth by respecting and learning from four sources of knowledge: the Bible, personal experience, Christian tradition, and reasoning. For him, the Bible came first, yet it needed to be balanced with the other three. (This came to be called "Wesley's quadrilateral.")

Tolerance as it's typically taught today is harmful because it undermines truth (reality), which is the foundation of life and morality. Empathy includes speaking the truth in love (Eph. 4:15).

4. **Empathy is not fixing.**

When Bill and I (Kristi) were newly married, we were both earning our doctorates in psychology, working full-time jobs to support ourselves and pay for school, and living at my grandparents' house to save money. One day we went to our bedroom to have some privacy, and I started crying about the pressure I felt with school, not liking my job, our finances, and the insecurity I felt in our relationship because Bill was so busy. My insecurity increased as I shared my emotions.

Bill listened and was quiet for a long time. I could tell he was thinking. I sat in the silence waiting, trying to hold back the shame I felt for my emotions and needs. Finally, he responded, "Kristi, it seems like about every thirty days you get overwhelmed and stressed and have heightened emotions. Have you considered that these feelings could be worse because of your hormone cycle?"

Bill's analysis was correct, but *I did not feel loved*. To make matters worse, he offered me some suggestions for how I might manage my stress better. I cried and withdrew, feeling even worse than when I first shared. Thankfully, he realized he'd hurt me and gently asked how he could support me. I replied, "I don't want to be fixed. I already know what I need to do. I just need to know I'm not alone; I need you to be a safe place for me to process my emotions and receive care."

Thankfully, Bill learned to give me empathy, putting caring words to what I was feeling. Ironically, when I felt deeply loved by him, I actually wanted to ask for his input!

5. **Empathy is not sympathy.**

Kristi and I (Bill) often find that people confuse empathy and sympathy. Typically, to give sympathy is to hear what someone shares and reply, "Oh, *I* feel the same way. That's how *I* felt when . . ." Whereas to give empathy is to hear what someone shares and reply, "I'm understanding *you* feel . . . Tell me more about that." If you give sympathy to people, you're probably enmeshing with them, overidentifying with what they feel, and putting the focus on your emotions. This tends to shut down their emotions and leave them feeling pressured to take care of *you*! In contrast, when you give people empathy, you stay calm to receive what they need to share, and you stay focused on understanding and caring for their emotional needs.

When Ryan was in college his father died. After the memorial service, a relative saw him and, intending to offer comfort, she cried, "Oh, I'm so sorry! This is so devastating!" and burst into tears. She hugged him and collapsed into his arms. Ryan stiffened up and began comforting *her*. The relative gave sympathy. She was so emotionally identified with Ryan's grief that her own grief gushed out like a geyser on him. He closed up his emotions and tried to help her. She lacked self-awareness and boundaries.

On the other hand, if you offer sympathy to a hurting friend by briefly sharing your similar experience and then give them empathy, putting the focus back to their felt need, it can be an effective expression of care.

6. **Empathy is not parroting words.**

There is a lot more to empathy than just listening—it's *how* we listen. If we repeat back the exact words someone said, then we'll come across like a parrot. The substance of empathy is not our word choices—it's the *intention of our hearts* to understand someone's situation and their thoughts and feelings about it. We're investing energy to feel *for* and *with* people through our heart, face, tone of voice, and words that validate their emotions. When you're listening to someone, you want to do your best to reflect back fresh feeling words you think they'll relate to, but even if you share the "wrong" words, it's fine because it gives them a chance to clarify. For example, "It's not that I feel disrespected by him—it's that I feel *abandoned*." Then you can reply, "Oh, I see. You're wanting to feel that you are not left alone." Then the person can elaborate, "Yes. For instance . . ."

7. **Empathy is not excusing sin.**

One day Kristi and I (Bill) were teaching on empathy and J.B., a pastor from the Bible Belt in America, questioned, "What about sin? In my ministry of discipleship, I

> need to correct people. I don't understand where empathy fits in. I certainly don't want to give empathy for sin." I replied, "Actually, your disciples do need empathy for their sins." This set him back in his chair. Then I explained myself and we discussed the issue.
>
> J.B.'s tradition was to confront the sin. Most of the time, the best *first response* to someone struggling with sin is to have an empathetic conversation to understand the person's situation, emotions, and needs and discern what the Spirit of God is doing in their life. Then you can graciously and conversationally address the sin and its consequences, seeking to gently restore people (Gal. 6:1). It's the kindness of the Lord that brings us to repentance (Rom. 2:4).

For each of the seven common misconceptions of empathy, we contrasted false empathy with true empathy that is both gritty and gracious. The following table summarizes these differences.

False Empathy vs. True Empathy

FALSE EMPATHY	TRUE EMPATHY
Coddles (indulges) emotions and desires	Lovingly challenges destructive beliefs and behaviors
Reassures (cheerleads) to generate positive feelings	Identifies and validates distressed emotions
Tolerates what is not true and idolizes emotions	Acknowledges any conflicts between emotions and truth
Tries to fix people with advice or insights	Facilitates learning and taking responsibility
Sympathizes by projecting your own emotions	Cares for and reflects others' emotions

FALSE EMPATHY	TRUE EMPATHY
Parrots back the same words that were shared	Warmly uses fresh words to reflect others' feelings
Excuses sin to give false comfort	Expresses concern about sin and its effects

The Power of Empathy

Even the CIA has learned the power of empathy! Recently, three CIA intelligence officers taught on empathy in a MasterClass lesson. One of them stated, "I think people would be surprised to learn how important empathy is at the CIA. . . . Empathy as a CIA officer . . . is just absolutely essential."[2] *True empathy makes everything in life better.* Every conversation with others, every job, every challenging situation, every Instagram post, every teaching opportunity, every discipleship program, every conflict resolution, every business meeting, and every prayer goes better with empathy. Obviously, empathy is crucial to spiritual direction and other helping relationships. For instance, a meta-analysis of dozens of research studies on psychotherapy found that an empathetic relationship between the therapist and client is the key to effective therapy.[3]

Henri Nouwen often described empathy as "care" and claimed that *care is the cure*. He writes, "Care is being with, crying with, suffering with, feeling with. . . . It is claiming the truth that the other person is my brother or sister, human, mortal, vulnerable, like I am."[4] He taught that if we rush in to fix people it's insulting to them, even *violating*. Instead, we can learn to stop trying to control other people and trust the sovereign Lord. In family, work, conflict resolution, and all of life, *giving and receiving empathy requires putting relationships first and leaving the results to God.*

Empathy is especially powerful as one of three essential ingredients in personal growth. Like how plants need water, sunshine, and soil to grow, so also you and the people you interact with need empathy, truth, and responsibility to grow. We can summarize this in a general "formula" for growth:

Empathy + Truth + Responsibility = Growth

Let's define our terms:

- **Empathy** is understanding, validation, and fellow feeling.
- **Truth** is insight, guidance, and boundaries.
- **Responsibility** is doing what is good and loving.

If any one of these three nutrients is removed, it stunts our growth and hinders our ability to abide in the love of the Father and the Son that we long for (John 15:9–10).

- Empathy without truth is inaccurate.
- Empathy without responsibility is coddling.
- Truth without empathy is harsh.
- Responsibility without empathy is drudgery.

But when the three are kept together the results are life-giving!

- Empathy helps truth be gracious.
- Empathy helps responsibility be joyful.
- Truth helps empathy be accurate.
- Responsibility helps empathy build courage.

> We list empathy first in our general formula for growth not because it's better but because it prepares the way for us to receive truth and act responsibly. In fact, the best empathy generates clear thinking that guides us in what is true and energizes us to act with love for God, others, and ourselves.

Holy Spirit's Ministry to You

In Romans 8, Paul teaches that Holy Spirit ministers God's empathy and truth to:

Set you free from sin (v. 2)
Govern your mind with God's peace (v. 6)
Give life to your body (v. 11)
Remind you that God is your Papa (v. 15)
Help you with your weaknesses (v. 26)
Listen to your longings (v. 27)
Search your heart (v. 27)
Pray for you according to God's will (v. 27)

When the Word of God meets your personal needs, it helps you to trust and know that you really are deeply loved by God.

Four A's of Empathy to Strengthen You

Jesus' conversation with the Samaritan woman at the well (John 4:1–26, 39–42) illustrates the power of the Four A's of Empathy when they are connected to truth and responsibility.

1. **Ask** questions

   Our Lord was curious, witty, and winsome in using questions to draw her into a personal and spiritual conversation. He did not shy away from a touchy subject. Instead, he spoke the truth in love, starting with asking about her broken marriages that had caused her much shame.

2. **Attune** to emotions

   Jesus tuned in to her hidden spiritual thirst for living water and her desire to worship God freely in spirit and truth. He helped her feel these spiritual longings, think about what was true, and take responsibility to act wisely rather than staying stuck as a victim and hiding from people. She was inspired to soften her heart to Jesus, ask him to satisfy her thirst, and trust him as her Messiah.

3. **Acknowledge** the significance

   Jesus drew out and validated the importance of her deep needs for true forgiveness, acceptance, and freedom to worship God. She became motivated to rethink her approach to her life and act responsibly by making the most important decision of her life to become a follower of Jesus.

4. **Affirm** strengths

   The Samaritan woman felt so affirmed and encouraged by Jesus that she went from being shamefaced and isolated from her community to daring to believe the truth that she had dignity as a Samaritan (mixed race) woman because the Messiah had befriended her (see the empathy practice on the next page). With confident joy she ran to tell everyone in her village that they needed to meet Jesus the Messiah!

EMPATHY PRACTICE:

Friendship with Jesus

A friend gave me (Bill) a photo printed on wood called *Christ and His Friend*. It's a replica of an icon painted in the eighth century in Egypt. It shows Jesus Christ standing with a calm smile, holding the book of the Gospels, and putting his arm around a friend standing beside him.[5] Jesus has one eye looking at his friend and the other looking straight ahead.

When we look at Jesus he says, "Now remain in my love . . . so that my joy may be in you. . . . I no longer call you servants. . . . Instead, I have called you friends, for everything that I learned from my Father I have made known to you" (John 15:9–15). Henri Nouwen translated the Greek word for "remain" (or "abide") as "make your home in."[6] *Jesus is inviting us to make our home with him in his Father's love.* The power to do works of love for others with joy is to find our home in the love of our Savior and Friend.

As I write to you, I have a photo of the icon *Christ and His Friend* on my desk. When I struggle to find the right words to share with you, I look into Jesus' loving face and meditate on his words in John 15. This reminds me to breathe and smile because I am deeply loved by Jesus. Then with Jesus I look out from the picture at you reading this book and pray for you to know that you are deeply loved by your Friend. (As I look at the picture, Jesus has one eye on me and one eye on you.)

I pray for you to receive Holy Spirit's words of empathy and encouragement. I pray for you to feel Jesus' arm around you and to know that the Lord Jesus is truly your friend. He is with you. His Father is your Father. He is helping you in your work and in all you do.

Reflection and Prayer

This guided prayer can help you engage Jesus' friendship in your work:

> Identify a work of love that you want to do with Jesus . . .
>
> Imagine yourself as Jesus' friend and you are doing this work together . . .
>
> Slowly repeat the Breath Prayer "Jesus calls me friend . . . I'm not alone . . ."
>
> As you breathe in, pray "Jesus calls me friend . . ."
>
> As you exhale, pray "I'm not alone . . ."
>
> *Smile!* It's true. Jesus is with you and is helping you to love others.

SOUL TALK

1. In what ways do you think empathy can become coddling?
2. What is one misconception of empathy that you've struggled with or been hurt by? How do you feel about this?

3. What is helpful for you about Wesley's quadrilateral that identifies four sources of knowing truth (Scripture, tradition, reason, and experience)?
4. What is an example of a relationship in which you experienced empathy and truth helping you be responsible and grow spiritually?
5. How does it feel for you to partner with the Lord in a work of love while praying "Jesus calls me friend . . . I'm not alone"?

PART TWO

Our Need for Empathy

Most of us have a personal struggle that holds us back from the flourishing life that we want and that God intends for us. The most common ones we see are worrying, feeling hurt by people, being triggered by emotional trauma or another stressor, reacting in anger, or getting drained from caring for people. No one wants to feel distressed in these ways, yet trying to ignore these emotional challenges just makes them worse—it keeps the care of God and other people at a distance.

In each of these five struggles, when you open up to your distressed emotions and ask for empathy from Jesus and safe people, you can experience the deeper love of God that you long for. This requires growing in self-awareness, which we help you with through examples of people you'll relate to, self-assessments, and insights from Scripture and psychology. Then we guide you in how to grow in emotional and spiritual health through our proven four-step model (the Four A's of Empathy) and a variety of empathy practices that guide you in how to receive comfort and strength from the Lord Jesus.

In the last chapter we help you learn how to steward your empathy and care for other people without it draining your soul. You'll discover that empathy empowers compassion, forgiveness, reconciliation with God and others, and fruitful work.

As in part 1, each chapter ends with an empathy practice and soul talk questions for you and your friends. The empathy practices are mindful prayer to calm worry, visual meditation to comfort hurts, Calming Touch Prayer to calm emotional triggers, praying an angry psalm to govern anger with love, and soul care with Jesus to not get drained by caring for others.

As you read these next chapters, we hope you will be able to say, "This expresses how I feel and what I need, and now I have words and hope for how I can grow. I want to share this with my friends so we can understand each other and follow Jesus together."

6

Releasing Worries

> Worry can rob you of happiness, but kind words will cheer you up.
>
> Proverbs 12:25 GNT

Most of us can testify that worry has robbed us of happiness, just as the proverb above says. Worry takes us away from enjoying moments of love, beauty, and goodness. Instead of savoring blessings, we worry about what is wrong or might go wrong.

Jesus may have had worries. He certainly was not a *chronic worrier*, but it's hard to imagine that as a human being thoughts of worry never entered his mind. For instance, he may have experienced worried thoughts when he was a child and his family escaped King Herod's plot to murder him (Matt. 2:13–18), when Satan tempted him in the wilderness (Matt. 4:1–11), when the religious leaders were trying to kill him before it was his time to go to the cross (Mark 3:6), or when his disciples were slow to learn his teachings (Matt. 15:16; 16:9, 11). In the Garden of Gethsemane, right before he went to the cross, we know he was "deeply distressed and troubled," and this surely included having worried thoughts (Mark 14:33).

> *Jesus, you are the Human One who feels for me when worry grips me. Please teach me and strengthen me to release my worries to your Father and return to peace, as you always do.*

I Was Besieged with Worry

One of the hardest things I (Bill) have done in my life was when Kristi and I led our Soul Shepherding ministry through a pivot from ten years of being a mom-and-pop ministry to becoming an organization that grew over 50 percent per year in the next five years. Today this includes fourteen full-time staff and over fifty who are part-time. It's been an honor and joy, but it's also been stressful, especially when we started the pivot.

My personality depends on knowledge and competence, but I worried that I didn't have the expertise I needed and was not a good enough CEO. Often worries buzzed in my head like bees—even at night. It seemed like every day there were new problems. I worried that I was not making the right strategic decisions, not leading our staff well, not networking enough, and missing opportunities. I worried that our expenses would outrun our revenue, especially because if I failed it would be public. I worried about disappointing Kristi and our board, staff, and donors who had given so much for this ministry.

I struggled with worry in my twenties and thirties but thought I had resolved this in my early forties when I learned how to release my worries to God and live in Jesus' easy yoke (Matt. 11:28–30). This message was so helpful to me and the people we ministered to that I wrote the book *Your Best Life in Jesus' Easy Yoke.* But after fifteen years of experiencing deeper peace and joy in Jesus, it seemed that in my new challenge as an organizational leader the easy yoke was slipping away. Our ministry helps pastors, missionaries, and others avoid burnout. I worried, *What if I burn out?*

I wanted to feel at ease all the time, but I learned that *Jesus' easy yoke was an easy way to do hard things.* His easy way was releasing my worries to him by seeking empathy, lowering my unreasonable self-expectations, collaborating more with others, and trusting him to carry the weight of leadership. In this way, over time, my worries were diminishing and my peace was increasing.

We All Have Worries

The average person has 70,000 thoughts a day, and many of them are negative. It seems our minds have Velcro for negative thoughts and worries but Teflon for positive thoughts.

Like many people we talk with, maybe you worry about doing a good job, getting all your work done on time, satisfying your clients, or meeting your boss's expectations.

We may find ourselves worrying about big things like wars or little things like parking places. We may worry about not having enough money to take care of our needs. We may worry about the well-being of our family and friends. We may worry about being criticized or judged by people. We may worry about people judging us. We may worry about getting older, declining health, dying, or being left alone.

Probably we know we can't control our circumstances and need to release our worries to God, but sometimes the bony fingers of worry grab hold of us and it's hard to peel them off.

Worry Assessment

One study found that 70 percent of people struggle with worry.[1] How about you? What is your experience with worry? Our Worry Assessment will help you understand to what extent you deal with worry. Answer each question below as *mostly true* (T) or *mostly false* (F). Mostly true means "Often I experience this."

1. I keep worrying about what might go wrong. T F
2. I get tired of overthinking situations. T F
3. My mind keeps worrying and it's hard for me to focus. T F
4. I get worried about my performance. T F
5. My worries cause me to avoid situations that I need to face. T F
6. I try to push worries out of my mind but it's hard to stop them. T F
7. I find myself worrying about what other people think of me. T F
8. When I go somewhere, I have recurring worries about staying safe. T F
9. I worry over and over about making mistakes. T F
10. I keep worrying about my health even after a doctor reassures me. T F
11. I keep anticipating worst-case scenarios. T F
12. My thoughts keep dwelling on situations that stress me. T F

13. I worry about the well-being of my loved ones. T F

14. I worry about whether or not I'm doing things the right way. T F

15. Worrying about things makes it hard for me to get a good night of sleep. T F

Each question you answered as "mostly true" indicates a need for empathy.

If you responded "mostly true" to six or more examples of struggling with worry, consider talking with a Soul Shepherding spiritual director or coach who can give you empathy, teach you relaxation techniques, and pray for you. Visit SoulShepherding.org/DeeplyLoved or scan this QR code.

A research study on chronic worriers found that *91 percent of the things they worried about did not come true*![2] That's a clear statement that worrying is a waste of time. Worse, chronic worrying chokes out God's invitation to participate in his kingdom of righteousness, peace, and joy (Mark 4:19; Rom. 14:17). But to stop worrying is much easier said than done. Just now, you've taken a first step to engaging the peace of Christ by reflecting on your experience with worry. A good next step is to understand the psychology of worry.

The Psychology of Worry

What does it mean to worry? How would you describe it? I looked up *worry* in several dictionaries and could not find an adequate definition. They all equated worry with anxiety. The two are different but often go together. If you have a thought of worry, it may be that you are not anxious; but if you are spinning in worry, then it indicates you have underlying anxiety, which is often unconscious. Both worry and anxiety feature distressed thinking, but strictly speaking, worry is not emotional, whereas anxiety is both emotional and mental (see the table below). To worry is to have recurring troubled thoughts that splinter your mind in different directions so that you can't think straight. Worry quickly becomes like a runaway train of obsessive thoughts. It can make you skittish, jittery, and jumpy—like a cat on a hot tin roof.

Generally, worry is distressed *thoughts* buzzing in your head while anxiety is distressed *emotions* churning in your gut. Worry is mostly conscious, but anxiety is mostly unconscious. Worry projects anxious emotions into external problems like a messy house and then cleans the house, as if that would solve the internal worry problem. Anxiety internalizes stressors from the environment, and then it becomes an upset stomach. Worry is like a scratch on a record that makes a line keep repeating over and over, whereas anxiety is like static on the radio because the station is not tuned in. Both can bring temporary relief—worry by solving external problems and anxiety by repressing emotions. But they don't bring real relief: Worry exhausts your mind and anxiety erodes your mental and physical health.

Worry vs. Anxiety

WORRY	ANXIETY
Distressed thoughts	Distressed thoughts *and emotions*
Mostly conscious	Mostly unconscious
Externalizes anxiety into your environment	Internalizes stress into your gut
Focuses on specific problems	Generalizes from many problems

WORRY	ANXIETY
Like a broken record (keeps repeating)	Like static noise on a radio
Solving problems brings temporary relief	Repressing emotions brings temporary relief
Causes mental fatigue	Causes health problems

Unfortunately, many Christians misinterpret the Bible's teachings on worry in ways that undermine healthy discipleship to Jesus and emotional maturity.

Biblical Misinterpretations About Worry

"Be strong and courageous" (Josh. 1:9) is misused to shame people for feeling fear.

"Do not worry" (Matt. 6:25) is misused to judge worry as sinful.

"Don't be afraid; just believe" (Mark 5:36) is misused to deny fear and profess faith.

"Do not be anxious" (Phil. 4:6) is misused to deny anxious emotions that need care.

The truth is that "Do not worry" is not a commandment or law—it's Jesus' *teaching*. The Greek word for *worry* that Jesus uses means "pulled in different directions at once" or "torn to pieces."[3] *Jesus is empathizing* with our experience of worry and inviting us to trust God's care. When the Master himself was in the shadow of the cross, besieged with worry and sinking in emotional turmoil, he trusted God as his dear Papa (Mark 14:36 MSG). He wants us to know God as our dear Papa too.

Consider our following paraphrase of Jesus' empathetic and wise teaching on worry:

> Do not keep worrying about food and money—your mind will get torn to pieces and you'll feel yanked all over the place. . . . Listen to the birds and see how your Papa in the heavens feeds them. . . . Do not keep worrying about your clothing and your image that people see. Look at the flowers and see how God clothes them so beautifully. . . .
>
> Your Papa in the heavens is nearby and wants to take care of all your needs. . . . Ask Papa for what you need. He's right beside you, and he loves to give good gifts to you. (Matt. 6:25, 26, 28; 7:7–9)

Our Lord is not saying it's a sin to have thoughts of worry (or feelings of anxiety). He is teaching us that *continually worrying* is a mental disease that can lead to distrusting God. In other words, having worried thoughts or anxious feelings is not a sin in itself, but it can lead to sin (Ps. 139:24). When you have worried thoughts or anxious feelings, Jesus does not look at you with a furrowed brow of judgment and he does not give you the simplistic advice to "Just stop it!" That's shaming, which pressures you to deny your struggles. Instead, Jesus is kind and empathetic toward you when you are under stress and worrying. *He woos you out of worry and into the wonder that right now your heavenly Father is caring for you "in secret"* (Matt. 6:4, 6, 18). Just as Papa cares for the flowers and birds, so also he cares for you and me. He is with us and helps us to not be controlled by worry.

Cycle of Worry

Let's delve deeper into understanding worry and how it relates to anxiety. The Cycle of Worry illustrated below identifies the dynamics of worry.

Stress

Stress comes from external events such as heavy responsibility, relational conflict, rejection, change, trauma, or an upsetting memory. Stress tempts us to worry.

Worry

Worried thoughts tend to multiply. When worrying becomes ruminating, it's like a runaway truck speeding downhill with no brakes.

Bodily Distress

Chronic worrying includes bodily distress (unconscious anxiety) that negatively affects your physical health. It puts your body in the fight, flight, or freeze mode, which increases the production of the stress hormones cortisol and adrenaline. You're likely to experience physical symptoms like antsiness, shallow breathing, rapid heart rate, sweating, churning in your stomach, tightness in your muscles, headaches, backaches, or sleep problems. Additionally, chronic worry and repressed anxiety can cause a weakened immune system, asthma, digestive illness, arthritis, chronic pain, obesity, diabetes, and heart disease.

Anxiety

Typically, anxiety and other distressed emotions hide under worry. Anxiety *is* repressed emotion; you feel anxious when you've been trying not to feel "negative" emotions like fear, anger, shame, or sadness.[4] But *what you resist will persist*. Denying distressed thoughts and emotions makes you more distressed. Chronic (habitual) anxiety puts you on pins and needles and can lead to decreased cognitive abilities, decreased creativity, and decreased capacity to enjoy experiences. Anxiety habits come from a combination of biology, anxious emotions you've absorbed from others (especially as a child), and unhealthy coping behaviors.

Unhealthy Coping Behaviors

To keep distress at bay we are likely to develop unhealthy habits like excessive planning, mindlessly scrolling on our phones, obsessively cleaning stuff, codependently helping people, fixating on problem-solving, overworking, hurrying, drinking alcohol, or engaging in sin. Unhealthy coping mechanisms don't truly alleviate worry, anxiety, or bodily stress symptoms, so the whirring wheel of worry keeps going round and round.

Trying to Control Things

Worry is trying to control situations, your image, your emotions, or other people. Ironically, as the Cycle of Worry illustrates, chronic worrying spins your life out of control and splits your soul into a public high-functioning self and a hidden anxious self. It's one of the ways we may become "two-souled" (James 1:8; 4:8 YLT), which we refer to as developing a *soul split.* It's like driving with one foot on the gas and the other on the brake, which grinds your engine. For instance, it's appropriate to feel scared or angry when something threatens your well-being, but if the unconscious defense mechanism of repression puts the brakes on, then you become anxious. Feeling fear and resisting fear splits your soul and wears down your body.

For instance, struggling with panic attacks is an anxiety disorder that indicates a painful soul split. Over the years we've talked with many people who have suffered through one or more panic attacks. Typically they say, "I don't know why it happened. I was doing fine." We ask them to tell us about their recent days and weeks, and out comes a string of five or six events that were stressful, and in each case they diminished their emotions and diverted their energy into overfunctioning in their work or relationships. They were out of touch with their own inner self. They were just skimming across the surface of their life and not realizing they had hidden deeper distressed emotions.

They had a panic attack because they forced a lid on top of their boiling emotions of anxiety, and finally the increasing pressure blew the lid off. (Other soul splits include stress reactions, habits of sin, angry outbursts, being overcome by tears in an unsafe situation, and addictive behaviors.)

Empathy for Your Thoughts

I (Kristi) like to ask Bill, "Penny for your thoughts?" He is a thinker, and I like to know what is going on in his head. When he shares his thoughts with me, usually some feelings come along too. This is especially important for worries since they are thoughts that often include undercover emotions of anxiety. With worry, as in all areas of human experience, we need empathy not only for our feelings but also for our thoughts.

Even for me as a feeler, I need empathy for my thoughts. Recently, Bill and I were on a ministry trip in Arizona near where I grew up, and I had lots of spontaneous memories from my childhood, which included my mother, who had died six months earlier. At that time, I wasn't aware of needing empathy for my emotions; I just wanted to verbalize my memories. I asked Bill if he could listen to me. His curiosity and questions helped me to process my thoughts in a stream of reflections. Then some underlying emotions related to my grief did bubble up for me, like laughter, sadness, warm appreciation, and love. Seeking empathy for my thoughts led to seeking empathy for my feelings. If I had held back my reflections on my childhood, it would've generated worry and anxiety from denying my grief. That would've diminished my enjoyment of God's presence and care during our trip to Arizona and my trip down memory lane. This is an example of why Scripture teaches us that in times of difficulty it's especially important to remember God's works of love (Ps. 143:5).

C. S. Lewis was an intellectual and an acclaimed scholar, yet he did not stay stuck in his head—he knew the importance of empathy. In *The Problem of Pain* he shared his conviction that knowledge would provide some help for his readers' pain, a little courage more help, a little human empathy even more help, and a tiny tincture of God's love more help than anything else.[5]

A client's face was frozen in worry. He had symptoms of anxiety like water-bugging thoughts, gut distress, being in a hurry, and irritability. He told me (Bill), "I can't feel my emotions. The closest I can get is to imagine what I might feel. I'm in my head all the time; I don't feel my emotions—*I think them.* They're just words filling up an empty void."

As I shared in chapter 2, many years ago I did not know what emotions I was feeling either. Whenever someone asked how I was feeling, I had no idea. Learning the language of emotions and how to ask for and receive empathy helped me learn to release my worries to God. I learned that *the way to stop worrying starts with asking for empathy.* I talked freely about my circumstances that worried me and discovered I had emotions that were hiding under my worrying. For instance, I might say, "I'm stressed." But when I verbalize my inner experiences with someone who is giving me empathy, I can elaborate, "It's like my stomach is tied up in knots." Processing your thoughts and feelings with a good listener helps you go deeper into your heart, like peeling back the layers of an onion.

That's how it works for you to calm down worrying by verbalizing your thoughts and feelings and receiving empathy. Some people are blessed to receive empathy as children, but many of us, as was true for me, need to start the empathy journey as adults. First, we need to rein in our habit of trying to relieve worries by solving external problems. Then, if we are emotionally vulnerable with God and safe people and we receive empathy, it will help us let go of worrying and relax in God's peace.

Releasing Your Worries in Prayer

Recently I (Kristi) had sinus pain the week before we'd be traveling to a 350-acre ranch in Texas to lead our Soul Shepherding Institute. I worried, *Oh no. Am I getting sick? Will I be able to lead our retreat? If I can't, how will Bill do it all without me? Which of our spiritual directors can I call to fill in for me?* Instead of ruminating in worry, I turned my worries into prayer.

I asked a friend to listen to me with empathy and pray for me.

I sent a prayer request to the prayer team that supports our ministry.

I prayed about my fear of getting sick and not being able to minister.

I asked God to strengthen my immune system and took immune booster nutrients.

I practiced mindful prayer to rest in the peace of God.

In all these ways I received three-way empathy from God, other people, and myself. I am thankful to say that I felt cared for and I did not get sick!

I was putting into practice Paul's prescription for worry:

> Don't worry about anything; instead, pray about everything; tell God your needs, and don't forget to thank him for his answers. If you do this, you will experience God's peace, which is far more wonderful than the human mind can understand. His peace will keep your thoughts and your hearts quiet and at rest as you trust in Christ Jesus. (Phil. 4:6–7 TLB)

Worry inflates problems. If I had dismissed my worries, that would've been rejecting the part of me that was worrying and needing security and care. Then worry would start converting into increasing anxiety and shame. *Empathy for worry rightsizes your worries*—it shrinks them down because you're releasing them to your almighty Savior. It gives you perspective, grace, and confidence. It quiets the static in your head and opens your mind to think clearly and see solutions. It helps you hang on the Lord's arm of omnipotence, trusting that in all situations, including suffering, he loves you and is working things out for you according to his good, pleasing, and perfect will (Rom. 8:28; 12:1–2).

Four A's of Empathy for Worry

When my (Bill's) stress and temptations to worry ramped up as an organizational leader, I needed empathy from Jesus, Kristi, my friends, and myself to release my worries to God. The statements below illustrate how I used the Four A's of Empathy to grow in peace. You can use them as prompts for self-empathy or giving empathy to others.

1. **Ask** questions

   What happened to stress me?

   How is this stress affecting my body and physical activity?

   What are my worried thoughts saying to me?

2. **Attune** to emotions

   I'm spinning in worry.

   It upset me when ______ happened.

   Things feel out of control.

   My body feels tense in my ______.

   I feel anxious about ______.

   I'm afraid about ______.

3. **Acknowledge** the significance

   This is really big for me because I need ______.

   The timing is hard because it's coming on top of my stress about ______.

   Worrying is hindering my ability to ______.

4. **AFFIRM** STRENGTHS

I've taken a good step to articulate my worries and anxious emotions.

I'm thankful to be learning how to release my worries to Jesus and receive his peace.

EMPATHY PRACTICE:

Mindful Prayer

I (Bill) love books that connect me with people's real-life challenges and stir my devotion to Jesus. When I see a bookshop that sells old books, I feel magnetically pulled to go inside and browse. It's like a treasure hunt for me to read the titles, find one that interests me, hold it in my hands, start flipping through the pages, and buy it to bring it home. Many books have been truly life-changing for me, and I never know when I'll find the next one!

One time Kristi and I were hiking along the coast in central Oregon, and we chanced upon a Little Free Library box at the Heceta Head Lighthouse. I browsed the books on the two small shelves and found the *Bay Psalm Book*. It was the first book printed in America, published by the Puritans of the Massachusetts Bay Colony in 1640. Through their many hardships they sang and prayed these psalms in their churches. As I leafed through it, I imagined myself in a congregation of early settlers in the New World. The words of the Psalms and the waves of the ocean filled my being. My mind became quiet and calm as I savored God's beautiful and awesome presence.

That's an example of mindful prayer. I directed my thoughts to enjoy God in the present moment. This requires accepting any worried thoughts or anxious feelings without judgment and releasing each one to God like a helium balloon. As I did this, my thoughts, bodily sensations, and emotions became still, yet pulsated with a lively appreciation of God's blessings. (Even now I feel grateful as I recall this experience.)

Praying Scripture meditatively teaches us to center our thoughts and feelings on our Lord. The brain scans of Franciscan nuns showed that when they meditated on God's love, the joy and peace centers of their brains lit up.[6] Your brain is moldable like plastic, so if you practice mindful prayer, you can develop neural pathways to experience God's joy and peace and ward off worry. Mindful prayer is the opposite of busy-brained worry that fragments our thoughts and feelings.

Let's take a minute to try mindful prayer with the *Bay Psalm Book* version of Psalm 23:1–3. Read the verses below and slowly to savor the words . . . Center your thoughts on a phrase you're drawn to and give thanks to your Shepherd . . .

> The Lord to me is a shepherd.
> Therefore I shall not want,
> In the folds of tender grass
> He causes me to lie down.
> To waters calm he gently leads,
> He restores my soul.[7]

If your thoughts are jumpy, try a simple brain hack for mindfulness like speaking a phrase of Psalm 23 out loud and slowly repeating it in prayer . . . In time God's words will seep down from your mind into your heart and bring you peace . . .

SOUL TALK

1. What were your results on the Worry Assessment? To what extent do you struggle with worrying?
2. What did you learn from the Cycle of Worry?
3. What is an example of you receiving empathy from God (through prayer or talking with a friend) that rightsized your worry?
4. Which of the Four A's of Empathy could be especially helpful for calming your worries?
5. Which line from Psalm 23:1–3 in the *Bay Psalm Book* were you drawn to? What do you feel about this?

7

Comforting Hurts

> Dear God, "I'm hurt and in pain; give me space for healing, and mountain air."
>
> Psalm 69:29 MSG

When we're hurting and in pain it can be hard for our souls to breathe. That is David's experience in Psalm 69 (MSG). He feels:

swamped (v. 2),
knifed in the back (v. 4),
hope in God (v. 6),
ashamed (v. 7),
shunned and unwanted (v. 8),
madly in love with God (v. 9),
sad-faced (v. 11),

sucked down into a black hole (vv. 14–15),
in trouble (v. 17),
caught in a death trap (v. 18),
kicked around (v. 19),
broken and without a shoulder to cry on (v. 20),
angry (v. 24),
gossiped about (v. 26),
hurt and in pain (v. 29),
full of praise and thankfulness to God (v. 30),
glad (v. 32),
and listened to by God (v. 33).

If you look over this list of David's emotional experiences, you can see that as he vents his negative emotions to God he is increasingly able to breathe the fresh mountain air and feel positive emotions (vv. 6, 9, 30, 32, 33).

Jesus invoked Psalm 69, as did his apostles.[1] He felt all these emotions and more. He cried out to his Father and found the comfort and encouragement he needed. In your hurts and hopes, troubles and praises, Jesus feels for you with empathy and provides the care you need.

Dear Jesus, I see in the Psalms and in your life on earth that you experienced every hurt that I go through. Thank you for feeling for me and providing the comfort I need.

Feeling Unwanted

While I (Kristi) was writing this chapter, I had a dream about feeling hurt and rejected by friends. In my dream, I was helping my mom host a dinner party for forty people, including many women I knew. When we had finished preparing the food, I went to find a seat for the meal. There were lots of open seats, but no one wanted to make room for me. I went from one table to another asking if I could sit with them. Everyone shook their head and replied, "No. That seat is saved." No one would even look at me—*they looked right past me* as they excitedly waved and called out to their friends to come sit with them. The tables were full of women talking and laughing. I stood there alone.

It seemed no one wanted me to join them. My heart flooded with sadness and I awoke. Immediately, I started praying, "Lord Jesus, please heal my rejection wound. I am so weary of it. Thank you, Jesus, that you will never reject me. Help me live confident that I am wanted and loved . . ."

I felt led by Holy Spirit to share this dream with you because you or one of your loved ones may relate, and I want you to know that I feel the pain with you, and so does Jesus. *You are not alone.*

You may be thinking that you don't relate to struggling with hurt or rejection. That's what I (Bill) used to think about myself. When I became a father, I learned that when I was an infant my mother taught me to sleep through the night by leaving me alone to "cry it out." I cried till I learned that *no one was coming to hold me*. I was on my own. To this day tears do not come easily for me. I was very well loved by my parents in many ways, but that was a very hurtful parenting method that contributed to me shutting down my emotions.

I learned to defend against feeling hurt by being independent and self-sufficient. I played football, which toughened me up more. If I got a cut or a bruise, my attitude was, *It's nothing—I can just rub some dirt on it and get back on the field.* But my confident shell cracked in high school when I experienced rejection from some of my peers and again in college when I was persecuted and bullied on a job. As I shared in chapter 2, I learned to feel my emotions and needs when I was a senior in college and received empathy from my Christian psychology teacher. I came to realize that my heart and personality were more sensitive than I had previously thought.

We All Have Hurts

Jesus focused his teachings on love because we are all relational beings who need to give and receive love, and anything less than that hurts us (Mark 12:30–31; John 13:34). Feeling hurt by a loved one or anyone you respect can be emotionally dysregulating. Understanding how you've been hurt (or sinned against) and how you've hurt (or sinned against) other people is the beginning of empathy, which supports forgiveness and reconciliation with God and others. It's important to name these hurts.

It hurts to be emotionally vulnerable and to receive advice rather than empathy. It hurts to be rejected, betrayed, criticized, or judged. It hurts to be gossiped about or slandered. It hurts to be manipulated, used for selfish purposes, or mistrusted. It hurts when someone wrongs you and does not apologize. It hurts when loved ones are angry at you or don't want to resolve a conflict with you.

Perhaps the hardest hurt to face is to look in the mirror and see that *I* have hurt people, even those I love. Often we hurt people by being too busy or not expressing care. We need humility and Jesus' hand of mercy to help us confess our sins and give empathy to people we've hurt.

Mother Teresa knew that the worst disease human beings experience is to be unwanted, unloved, and uncared for. That's why she devoted her life to caring for the poorest of the poor who had been abandoned to die on the streets in Calcutta, India. She noted, "There are many in the world who are dying for a piece of bread but there are many more dying for a little love."[2] She founded the Missionaries of Charity, who to this day continue to minister the compassion of Christ to comfort people who are spiritually impoverished around the world.

Relational Wounds Assessment

We all need to love and be loved by our family and friends. Yet, a research study found that 74 percent of people do not feel belonging in their local community.[3] Our Relational Wounds Assessment will help you better understand what you feel in your relationships.

Answer each question below as *mostly true* (T) or *mostly false* (F). Mostly true means "Often I experience this."

1. When I feel criticized by someone significant to me, my mood plummets. T F
2. I tend to perceive conflict with a loved one as rejection. T F
3. When a loved one seems to reject me, I feel embarrassment or shame. T F
4. In my most important relationships I seek repeated reassurance that I'm secure. T F
5. I keep replaying in my mind social situations in which I felt unloved. T F
6. If a friend turns down my invitation, I fear being dropped as a friend. T F
7. When I feel unloved, I experience sudden and intense sadness. T F

8. When I've been rejected it feels like a stab to my heart—it hurts physically. T F
9. When a loved one is disappointed in me, I am my own harshest critic. T F
10. I try to please family and friends in order to feel accepted. T F
11. I'm slow to share my true self with people because I don't want to be judged. T F
12. When someone I trust rejects me, I feel sudden and intense anger. T F
13. On my birthday I'm sensitive to whether or not people show me love. T F
14. When someone does not return my call, I feel hurt. T F
15. I wish I was not so sensitive to rejection. T F

If you responded "mostly true" to six or more examples of struggling with relational wounds, consider talking with a Soul Shepherding spiritual director or coach who can give you empathy and ministry such as healing prayer. Visit SoulShepherding.org/DeeplyLoved or scan this QR code.

The Psychology of Relational Wounds

As a child I (Kristi) was often told by my parents not to cry or show other emotions. This was hurtful to me. My parents loved me and took good care of me in so many ways, but they were strong thinkers, and it seemed they did not want anything to do with my emotions. For instance, when I was a little girl, my older sisters and parents were hiking to a special place to take a photo for our family Christmas card. The snow was so deep that I sank up to my thighs with every step. I couldn't keep up and became frightened that I'd be left behind and buried in the snow. I burst into tears. My dad finally came back to help me, but he seemed frustrated, and I felt hurt and ashamed. I felt too little, too slow, too weak, and too sensitive. *I hated myself for being so emotional.*

To make matters worse, when I was older I added salt to my wounds by misinterpreting Scriptures to reinforce my rejection and hatred of my emotions. I've talked to so many people who do this. Here are some examples:

Biblical Misinterpretations About Hurts

"Do not dwell on the past" (Isa. 43:18) is misused to deny past hurts that need care.

"The heart is deceitful" (Jer. 17:9) is misused to shame people for having emotions and desires.

"We rejoice in our sufferings" (Rom. 5:3 ESV) is misused to deny hurts and act happy.

"We walk by faith, not by sight" (2 Cor. 5:7 KJV) is misused to pit faith against emotions.

It's hurtful when friends or shepherds use Bible verses like these as Band-Aids to cover up emotional wounds or questions that need empathy. That's turning promises from God's Word into knickknacks (see Job 13:12 MSG). Instead, you need *mirror neurons of empathy*. The Bible teaches us to be slow to speak and quick to listen (James 1:19), to weep with those who weep (Rom. 12:15), and to offer compassion to others as Jesus does (Luke 6:36).

Along these lines, parents may tell their crying child things like, "It's okay. Don't cry." Usually this is said in an upbeat spirit or soft tone of voice, intending to reassure their child that nothing is wrong and they do not need to be upset. There is something nice and well-intentioned about reassurance, but usually *it invalidates the child's emotions*, as if there is no reason for them to feel that way. But there *is* a reason—even if the child's emotions are out of proportion to their circumstances, there are historical, relational, physical, personality, or emotional factors that do explain their emotions. Advice, judgment, and reassurance are contrary to empathy, and they put pressure on children (and adults) to deny their emotional needs and pretend. These responses contribute to emotional immaturity and difficulty trusting God.

All of us were sensitive to relational wounds as little children. We cried when we came out of our mother's womb. With raw emotion and no words or thoughts, we cried for food, warmth, comfort, holding, and bonding. We cried to be wanted, known, accepted, and loved. But if you did not receive comfort, you may have shut down your emotions. All our lives we have a biological and spiritual need to be securely attached to someone who gives us empathetic care. It's why when infants are startled they instinctively open their arms like they want to be held.[4] When you let yourself experience the need to be loved, you probably have some sensitivity to getting hurt—even if you are a thinker like Bill.

We all need to have our hurts and other distressed emotions listened to, understood, and cared for by someone in order to receive comfort. As we've been pointing out in this book, even Jesus needed empathy: "He prayed strongly and he cried loudly with many tears. . . . And God listened to Jesus" (Heb. 5:7 EASY). That's what God does for you. At least eight times in the Bible the Lord explicitly says that *when we cry out he hears us.*[5] That's heartfelt empathy. When we receive empathy, it supports us in developing the ability to return to joy after an upset, empathize with others, and trust in God.

Emotions are the natural language of the soul. They help us understand and love one another.

Cycle of Relational Wounds

We've identified a Cycle of Relational Wounds that can help you better understand the hurts that you and the people you care for experience.

Cycle of Relational Wounds

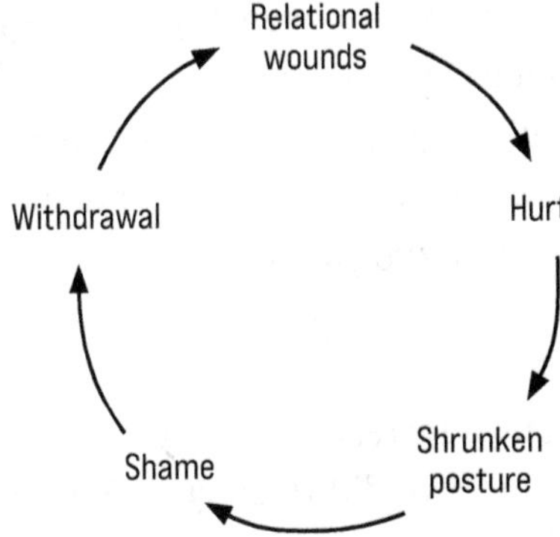

Relational Wounds

At times we all experience relational wounds like criticism, rejection, neglect, broken promises, manipulation, or abuse. They are especially damaging when they come from a loved one.

Hurt

It's natural to feel hurt, distressed, wronged, or sad when someone mistreats you or rejects you. In your body you may feel hurt feelings as watery eyes, a lump in your throat, or a heartache. If you deny your emotions or react to them, then the injury gets infected and doesn't heal.

Shrunken Posture

Experiencing rejection hurts like physical pain; the two are similar in your brain.[6] In other words, feeling rejection is not just social and emotional—it's *physical*. You probably feel the hurt in your body. It pulls you to go into hiding. Your eyes look away, your head drops, your body curls in and gets smaller, and you want to disappear.

Shame

Shame is not only an emotional response to sinning. You also feel shame when you've been rejected (or perceive that you've been rejected) by someone you trust. Feeling violated, downgraded, or guilt-tripped are other examples of shame. Ultimately, *shame is self-rejection*. It is probably the most painful emotion, kicking you when you're down.[7]

Withdrawal

Shame gets you to retreat into yourself by putting on fig leaves, as Adam and Eve did (Gen. 3:7). We may hide from other people and even our own selves through unhealthy coping mechanisms like people-pleasing, overeating, bingeing on social media, numbing emotions, overachieving, and alcohol dependence. The sad irony is that in doing so, we end up hiding from the empathy and care that God and safe people have for us.

Feeling Bible Truths

Samantha's voice trembled as she explained to me (Bill), "I'm trying to feel Jesus' words holding me, but I can't." She showed me a pencil drawing of a woman curled up in a ball. Her face was hidden behind her long hair, and she was surrounded by written phrases from the Bible that were moving toward her like rays of sunshine. I asked her to tell me about the picture and how she felt about it. She explained that it depicted that she was trying to receive comfort from Scripture but to her they were *just words*. The harder she tried to reason her way out of feeling hurt, the more she felt guilt and shame that reinforced her feeling rejected, so she was hiding from the words of Scripture that were meant to comfort her.

As I listened to Samantha, I was depending on the Spirit of Jesus to help me care for her. I wanted her to sense his deep, healing compassion, which had motivated the promises of Scripture that she'd been reciting to herself. I saw that Samantha's posture with me in the office was like her picture—she was crumpled in shame and hiding in fear. Yet, in response to my gentle questions and warmhearted concern, she had slowly lifted her head and peered into my soft eyes. Little by little, in our conversation that day and in subsequent conversations, she trusted that God was emotionally holding her and caring for her. The truths of God's Word came to life for her through experiencing them in a relationship of empathy and comfort. She was not rejected—she was deeply loved by Jesus.

A research study found that when people are experiencing rejection it dramatically reduces their IQ and reasoning abilities while increasing aggressive tendencies.[8] You've probably experienced this. When you are feeling hurt, your primary need is for empathy that provides validation and comfort—not teaching that devalues your emotions and not reassurance that pumps up false cheer. Imagine if whenever you felt rejected or hurt in any way you gave yourself empathy. Imagine if you and your friends did this for one another and other people who were hurting. Empathy for hurts fosters trust, emotional health, and loving relationships with God and one another. It also paves the way for gaining new insights and wisdom.

Empathy for Emotions, Not Perceptions

I (Kristi) have shared that I am sensitive to feeling hurt. I used to have a cat named Charlie who made me smile and laugh every day. He followed me around the house and made me feel wanted. He delighted to sit in my lap and be petted by me. I never felt lonely with Charlie nearby! I've had cats all my life and he was my very favorite. My daughter and I sobbed in grief when he died of old age. We then got a ragdoll cat because they are known for being affectionate. We named him Andy after Raggedy Andy. But he is rambunctious and aggressive. He does not even want to be touched, let alone held. Every day I try to pet him but he rejects me. I keep reminding myself he's not really rejecting me—he's just that kind of a cat! What I'm doing there is differentiating my perceptions from my emotions. The reason I feel hurt and rejected is because Andy's behavior strikes the nerve of my abandonment wound from childhood.

Over the years I have helped many people who blur their perceptions of other people and their emotions. Their emotions fixate on whether or not they are loved and included, and then they find themselves *anticipating that they will be judged or rejected by others*. They misinterpret social cues like bad moods, shyness, lack of enthusiasm, stress reactions, or busyness as indicators that they are not wanted when in fact that is not how the other person feels about them. In other words, they project their hurt emotions onto the other person. Then, feeling that they are on thin ice in the relationship, they keep seeking reassurance that they are accepted and loved. If this comes across as clingy, overwhelming, or blaming, then their actions may push away their loved one or provoke an angry conflict. In this way, fearing rejection becomes a self-fulfilling prophecy that leads to being rejected.

Projecting emotions often takes the form of "you" statements: "You make me feel unloved . . . You keep getting lost in your head . . . Why can't you be more considerate of me? . . . You're attentive to other people but not me . . . If you would stop doing whatever your boss wants . . ." Emotional projections like these often lead to emotional reactions, with each person ricocheting off the other. They also can lead to angry conversations in our heads and negative assumptions about people.

In relationships with others, your emotions are about you and your perceptions are about other people. Your emotions are your personal and embodied experiences; they are subjectively true for you, and you get to be the authority on saying what it is that you feel and need. Your perceptions are your interpretation of another person's behavior or motivations and are often inaccurate. Projecting, judging, blaming, cajoling, and reacting are unhelpful. If you blame other people or fall into a victim stance, it's unloving to others and it blocks your personal well-being and healthy intimacy.

Earlier in our marriage, Bill and I had conflicts like this. I would say to Bill something like, "I feel you don't want to be with me." Then he'd get defensive. I discovered this was because he felt judged when I verbalized my *perceptions of him* instead of owning that these were my emotions. After repeating this cycle many times and listening to and empathizing with what it was like to be him hearing this, I learned to communicate my emotions and needs with a request for his empathy along these lines: "I'm feeling insecure. Would you have time to listen to me and seek to understand what I am feeling?" Notice how I changed from making "you" statements (my negative perceptions of him) that put Bill back on his heels and instead communicated with "I" statements (my emotional needs) that invited Bill to step closer to me with empathy.

Your Sacred Wound

When we started Soul Shepherding in 2009, God winsomely challenged me (Kristi) to come out of hiding. My tendency was to stay on the sidelines to serve and cheerlead for Bill as he provided the teaching. One day out of the blue a woman came up to me and declared, "The Lord wants you to know that he sees you and that other people need your wisdom."

Jesus offered his wounds for our healing, and I could join with him by offering my relational wounds to help other people experience Jesus' healing touch in their hurts. As a teacher, when I was vulnerable to share my story, people thanked me and shared their experiences. They told me they had felt judged for being "too sensitive" or "too emotional" and not having "more faith." They experienced me as a safe place to share their emotions, tears, and questions and receive empathy. Hearing my story gave them courage to go deeper with Jesus on an inner journey of emotional healing and spiritual formation.[9]

Your deepest hurt can become your best blessing. That can be true for you if you learn to receive and give empathy. As disciples of Jesus, when we entrust our hurts to him, they can become sacred wounds that God repurposes to give comfort, health, and strength to others. Out of our brokenness God brings blessing to us and the people we care for. When we serve as wounded healers with Jesus, God gives us the honor of connecting heart to heart with people who have similar stories and hurts as our own, and we get to bless them out of the healing and redemption from the Lord that we have experienced (2 Cor. 1:3–7).

Four A's of Empathy to Comfort Hurts

The Four A's of Empathy have helped me (Kristi) process my emotions and receive Jesus' empathy and comfort when I feel rejected or hurt in another way. I invite you to try this with your hurts. You can use the empathy prompts below to receive comfort for your hurts and to comfort others who are hurting.

1. **Ask** questions

   What is happening in my life today that feels hurtful?

   Where am I feeling rejected or unwanted by someone?

2. **Attune** to emotions

   Yesterday, in my interaction with my friend I felt unseen and unappreciated.

   It hurt me when she ________.

   I felt sad that ________.

3. **Acknowledge** the significance

   Feeling rejected by my friend cut deep in my heart—it's a recurring wound.

   When I feel unwanted, I feel myself falling into shame.

   This injury is holding me back from _______.

4. **Affirm** strengths

   Jesus, I'm thankful for the comfort you give me.

   I'm encouraged by Scriptures like . . .

   With God's help I'm learning to . . .

EMPATHY PRACTICE:

Visual Meditation

When Bill and I (Kristi) were blessed with our first sabbatical, we spent time together resting in God, enjoying beaches and hiking in nature, and talking with our spiritual director. Each day we meditated on a different Gospel story in the life of Jesus, using our imaginations and praying through our emotions as we followed the three steps in our Ignatian Meditation Guides.[10] We journaled our prayers in solitude and silence. Then we met to share our experiences, give each other empathy, and pray together.

I invite you to use Ignatian meditation to visualize yourself with Jesus, feel your emotions, and receive his empathy. The three steps are to ask for grace, imagine being in the Gospel, and respond in prayer. Below I share an example to help you get started.

Zacchaeus Meets Jesus (Luke 19:1–10)

1. Ask for grace.

   Offer the Ignatian prayer, "God, our Lord, I desire the grace that you order all my thoughts, intentions, and actions to praise and serve you."

Lord God, I (Kristi) ask that you minister your grace and wisdom to me for my relational wound.

2. Imagine being in the Gospel.

   Read Luke 19:1–10 and visualize yourself in the story. Don't seek intellectual insights—stay with the imagery. Use your senses to see, touch, feel, and hear. What part of the story are you drawn to? Which character do you identify with, or are you a bystander?

   I was drawn to place myself in Zacchaeus' position. I related to him because, like me, he was short and felt rejected.

   I imagine Zacchaeus hearing the good news about Jesus, the prophet who heals the sick, feeds thousands, preaches with authority, and eats with people who are judged as "sinners" and others who feel rejected. He wants to see Jesus, but there's a thronging crowd of people from Jericho gathered at the road who have shunned and despised him for being a tax collector for the Roman government that oppresses them. All his worldly wealth, comforts, and distractions leave his soul empty. He feels judged, afraid, rejected, ashamed, alone.

   He recalls hearing that even the tax collector Matthew was accepted by Jesus. A ray of hope darts into Zacchaeus' heart: "Maybe Jesus would love me and welcome me into his community!" He gets the idea to climb up a tree along the street. He hides up there, peering through the leaves to look for Jesus. He's waiting and waiting, till finally he sees Jesus walking toward him on the road. Suddenly, Jesus sees him in the tree, calls him by name, and says he wants to come to his house for dinner! Zacchaeus' secret prayer has been heard. God has not judged or rejected him—he is seen and wanted by the Lord Jesus.

Zacchaeus is so excited, he jumps down from the tree, runs to Jesus, and walks home with him.

3. Respond in prayer.

Reread Luke 19:1–10 to experience the story in the role of the character God led you to. Then talk with the Lord. What do you feel? How does this relate to something in your life today? What is God saying to you?

Being in Zacchaeus' position in the Gospel story helps me to feel my own fears of not being loved by others, even God. When Jesus looks into my eyes and invites me to spend time with him, I feel surprised and thrilled. I feel honored to be chosen by Jesus. I feel thankful that God really is so good and loving—even to me, despite my tendency to hide for fear of being rejected.

Lord God, I confess that like Zacchaeus I try to secure myself with success in the eyes of others and pleasures like having nice things and eating sweet foods. But my deep longing is to belong to Jesus, be securely attached to him in true community, and serve you by shepherding others. Forgive me for when I doubt your goodness and loving presence.

Thank you, Father, that, as Jesus shows me, you always see me with eyes of grace, you feel empathy for me, and you choose to be in relationship with me. Even when I am hiding, your Spirit finds me and loves me. Thank you that you keep wooing me and training me to be indifferent to all worldly attachments so that I can love, praise, and serve you alone by being generous with others as Zacchaeus was. Amen.

SOUL TALK

1. Which emotion(s) in the list from Psalm 69 at the beginning of this chapter have you felt recently?
2. What were your results on the Relational Wounds Assessment? How do you feel about this?
3. What did you learn from the Cycle of Relational Wounds?
4. Which of the Four A's of Empathy could be especially helpful for comforting your hurts?
5. When you imagine yourself with Jesus in the Zacchaeus story, what do you feel?

8

Calming Emotional Triggers

> The Lord God is my strength.
> He makes me like a deer that does not stumble
> so I can walk on the steep mountains.
>
> Habakkuk 3:19 NCV

Some people say, "I've never experienced trauma. I haven't been abused or gone through a war." But often they have experienced some form of trauma and either they don't understand it as trauma or they're denying their emotional distress. Trauma triggers happen when you experience stress or hurt and it taps into the feelings and memories associated with a past trauma. You find yourself reliving the trauma and in urgent need of God's strength to be sure-footed like the deer.

What does it mean when someone says, "I got triggered"? Let's define some terms. An emotional trigger is an event that sneaks up on you and evokes a previous trauma or distress. The trigger itself may be as innocuous as something you smell, but it causes you to reexperience a past trauma, wound, or stressor. A trauma trigger is a type of emotional trigger that is more intense. All triggers cause emotional dysregulation that is difficult to calm down and is disruptive to your life and relationships. Examples of being dysregulated include low frustration tolerance, stress reactions, losing your temper, impulsive behavior, moodiness, or feeling overwhelmed by strong emotions.

We've been looking at our Lord Jesus as the Human One who can relate to all of our emotions and suffering. He may have experienced emotional triggers or similar distresses in situations like when his family kept rejecting him (Mark 3:21; 6:3–4; John 7:5), when Peter tempted him to avoid the cross just as Satan had done in the wilderness (Matt. 16:21–23; 4:1–10), or when the soldiers kept whipping him (Matt. 27:26). When you or a loved one are emotionally triggered or distressed, Jesus feels for you. He is with you and for you. In the frightening storm on the Sea of Galilee (Mark 4:37–38), Jesus felt the storm, calmed himself in his Father's care, and spoke his peace into his disciples and us: "Peace! Be still!" (v. 39 ESV). The Son of God is our strong and safe refuge.

Precious Lord Jesus, I recall the stories of your sufferings and your courage to feel the upsets, pain, and trauma and to keep relying on your Father for calm strength. I depend on you for the courage and calm that I need for my emotional triggers or stress reactions.

Trauma Triggers

Some years ago I (Kristi) experienced a trauma trigger after I was at the neonatal ICU to support my niece and her baby girl Grace, who needed heart surgery to survive. As an infant

I needed stomach surgery to keep me alive. I felt abandoned because my mom was not allowed to stay with me. Now, many years later, it was as if I was transported back in time to my infant self on the surgery table: *I'm cold and hungry. I'm all alone. I'm so scared. I can't help myself. A dark cloud is suffocating me. I'm losing my will to live. God, why is this happening to me?*

I could not have consciously formulated these feelings and thoughts as a baby, but now they flooded me. I did not know why. I did not realize my own trauma as an infant had been triggered.

I was in a quicksand of despair for a couple of hours. Bill asked me what I was feeling, and I didn't want to answer. It's strange, but I felt shame and hopelessness, like I didn't deserve to live and didn't even want to. I couldn't even make eye contact with him. I was listless. I wanted to curl up into a ball and go to sleep—*forever*. Looking back, it still surprises me that I fell into such a dark hole. I thought that after receiving therapy and healing prayer years earlier, I had been emotionally healed from this trauma and having it triggered. But visiting baby Grace in the ICU and being present to my niece's fears and tears took me back in time to what I felt in my own trauma.

Let's consider some examples of trauma triggers that you—or people you care for—may experience and need to receive empathy for in order to restabilize and heal.

- A friend was on a plane that had to make an emergency landing, and she developed post-traumatic stress disorder (PTSD) with flashbacks, chronic anxiety, and being too scared to fly again.
- A client was caring for her elderly father and reported, "All my childhood problems moved back in with me. I find myself walking on pins and needles like when I was a girl."

- A friend who is alcoholic and has a troubled relationship with his dad played tennis with him, and they had a conflict that triggered him emotionally, so he left abruptly and got drunk.
- A family member of this same friend has been burned by rescuing him in the past and reports that whenever she sees him, she keeps him at arm's length.
- Caught in a church conflict, a young pastor had the parent of one of his students yell at him, "You are the worst youth pastor in history!" These words became like arrows shooting at him in subsequent conversations with other parents.
- For over six months a counselor had been overloaded with the vicarious trauma of listening to and empathizing with her clients' traumas. She had to take a leave of absence and receive therapy so she could recover.

For many years I (Bill) did not think I had experienced trauma as a child. But I had trauma too, and my lack of awareness meant I was not receiving the empathy and care that I needed. In the previous chapter I shared that when I was a little boy my parents left me alone in my crib at night to "cry it out." Another trauma was that when I was five years old my parents often had me babysit my two-year-old sister while my mom drove my dad to the train station so he could go to work. I was so frightened—I had no clue how to be responsible for my baby sister. I acted like I was capable and buried my emotions and needs.

Whenever I felt rejected or judged, even as an adult, it touched my repressed memories that no one would respond to my cries, but I did not realize this. Instead of feeling my hurts and needs, I calloused my emotions, stiffened my back, acted strong and independent, and briskly walked away as I told myself, "I don't need them anyway." In these instances my trauma from being emotionally neglected as a child was triggered in ways that were emotionally dysregulating. For many years I did not connect my stress reactions to these triggers.

Traumatic experiences, whether they're intrusive violations or emotional neglect, damage your identity and steal your joy. They may cause overwhelming physiological and emotional arousal, lack of safety, and loss of ability to function well in your work or relationships. These painful effects may be immediate or delayed, short-term or long-term. Gaining new freedom and strength begins with identifying your emotional triggers.

Emotional Triggers

Often when someone says "I got triggered," what they are referring to is not a trauma trigger but an *emotional* trigger. Some emotional triggers are from experiencing trauma, but others come when an event strikes a nerve from a past hurt. You may get emotionally triggered when you experience grief, neglect, rejection, criticism, conflict, stress overload, or disappointment. When you interact with someone who feels difficult for you, they may say or do something hurtful that "pushes your buttons," which tempts you to react with hurt or anger. These emotional triggers are often not as severe as trauma triggers, but they can be very disruptive or painful. Emotional triggers and trauma triggers are always connected to memories that carry emotions. Often those emotional memories are implicit, which means they're recorded in your brain but you've forgotten or repressed them.

Past trauma or emotional wounds often get triggered by external circumstances such as engaging with a particular location, object, or event. For example, people who were sexually violated in the past may get triggered by a sexually graphic scene in a movie that causes them to feel violated in a similar way to how their younger self felt. In addition to sight, our other senses (hearing, smell, taste, and touch) can trigger painful memories and emotions. We also may get triggered by internal emotional states. For example, feeling depressed may trigger a past experience of being depressed that we relive.

Whatever their source, *triggers jump at you from the shadows and hijack your ability to enjoy moments and love others well.* This vulnerability can cause you to feel overpowered by flashbacks, bodily distress, or sluggishness. You may feel overwhelming emotions of fear, vulnerability, grief, anger, anxiety, shame, or loneliness. Sometimes when people are triggered they don't feel intense emotions because of their habits of denying their emotions and avoiding problems. Instead of feeling their emotional distress, they react unconsciously with an unhealthy coping behavior or stress reaction, which shows they were emotionally triggered.

Naturally, we'd like to think that putting faith in God would shield us from all trauma, injustice, and triggers, but often that is not the case. In the Bible we see many instances of God's children suffering from trauma and other painful wounds:

- Job was a righteous man, yet he went through devastating sufferings, each trauma triggering grief from the previous traumas (Job 1:13–2:10).
- Naomi was widowed and both her sons died—she could not shake her grief and became bitter and depressed (Ruth 1:20–21).
- David probably had nightmares when he was hiding in the desert from King Saul's army (Ps. 63:6–11).

- Tamar was raped by her half brother and endured public humiliation for the rest of her life (2 Sam. 13:12–20).
- Paul endured many harsh persecutions (2 Cor. 11:23–27).

As Jesus explained, "Here on earth you will have many trials and sorrows. But take heart, because I have overcome the world" (John 16:33 NLT).

Highly Sensitive Persons

Psychologist Elaine Aron's research studies showed that 20 percent of humans and animals are highly sensitive persons (HSPs) who are biologically wired to be highly sensitive and emotional, which makes them more vulnerable to getting emotionally triggered. There are four traits that HSPs have in common, which spell out DOES:[1]

1. *Depth of processing.* HSPs are deeply introspective and need time and space to process what they think and feel about situations. Before making a decision, they need to reflect, pray, talk to friends, weigh the pros and cons, or do some research. Their inner depth can inspire insight and creativity.
2. *Overstimulation.* HSPs have an especially permeable soul and are prone to absorb whatever stimuli is in their environment. They are quick to feel upset, anxious, angry, guilty, or emotionally overloaded. But on the positive side they are also quick to feel excitement, appreciation, peace, intimacy, and love.
3. *Emotional reactivity.* HSPs have deep and intense emotions, both pleasant and unpleasant. They are vulnerable

to getting triggered emotionally, being hurt by other people, and reacting to stress with tears, fear, frustration, or guilt. At the same time, their emotional nature is a gift that fosters empathy and intimacy.

4. *Sensitive to subtleties.* HSPs are highly sensitive to sounds, hot or cold temperatures, strong smells, coarse fabrics, and intense tastes. Stimuli that other people do not notice will be poignantly sensed by HSPs.

Some people mistakenly think the sensitivity of HSPs is an emotional dysfunction, but it's a normal characteristic of being high in the personality trait of sensory-processing sensitivity. In fact, HSPs have special gifts of empathy, emotional intelligence, communication, intuition, and creativity. The emotional and relational gifts of HSPs are validated by brain-imaging research that shows how, compared to other people, the mirror neurons of HSPs are more active in emotional and spiritual processing.[2]

Do you relate to some of the HSP traits? Would any of your family members or friends relate? Learning that I (Kristi) am an HSP has helped me receive empathy for my emotional sensitivities and stay out of shame. It's also helped me reflect empathy to others who are sensitive. I recall a client of mine who was an HSP. Before we started the session together, we were in the break room getting some tea. Suddenly, an adrenalized man charged in. His feet pounded on the wood floor as he was talking on the phone with a loud and brash voice. My client whisked herself out of the kitchen right away and hid in my office. When I sat down with her she explained, "I'm sorry, I just could not handle the energy coming off that man's body!" He was a lawyer who was arguing and fighting to defend his client. The force of his aggressive personality triggered her emotionally and utterly overwhelmed her.

Emotional Triggers Assessment

A worldwide research study found that 70 percent of people have experienced trauma.[3] As we've seen, if you have experienced trauma in the past, it is likely to get triggered at some later point—perhaps many times. It's like walking through a minefield. Probably all of us have experienced emotional wounds or griefs that lie dormant and may later be detonated.

What has been your experience with triggers? To what extent do you struggle with trauma triggers or other emotional triggers? Our Emotional Triggers Assessment will help you better understand what you feel in your life and relationships.

The questions below relate to whether or not you are being triggered by one or more traumatic or upsetting events from your past. Answer each question as *mostly true* (T) or *mostly false* (F). Mostly true means "Often I experience this."

1. I try to avoid upsetting situations that may trigger a past hurt or trauma. T F
2. Sometimes I find myself replaying past traumas or stressors I've experienced. T F
3. When something reminds me of a past trauma I feel depressed. T F
4. Sometimes I have upsetting dreams that relate to hurtful experiences from my past. T F
5. I never know when I might suddenly be reliving a past suffering I went through. T F
6. When I recall a past trauma, angry conflict, or hurt, it causes me bodily distress. T F

7. When a past trauma is triggered for me, I tend to withdraw from loved ones. T F
8. Movies that remind me of past wounds make me so upset it's hard to calm down. T F
9. When a painful memory is triggered for me it disrupts my sleep. T F
10. I avoid people, places, or things that are associated with past trauma or pain. T F
11. I scan my environment for possible dangers that might feel violating. T F
12. When someone gets angry at me, it shakes my insides and I just want to hide. T F
13. Sometimes I have intrusive and distressing memories about past hurts. T F
14. When a past violation is triggered for me, I become emotionally detached. T F
15. I get irritated by anything that upsets my sense of calm, peace, and safety. T F

If you responded "mostly true" to six or more examples of struggling with emotional triggers, consider talking with a Soul Shepherding spiritual director or coach who can give you empathy, teach you calming practices, and pray for you. Visit SoulShepherding.org/DeeplyLoved or scan this QR code.

The Psychology of Emotional Triggers

One day shortly after our oldest child, David, went off to college, I (Kristi) went into his room to get something and suddenly started to weep. His room felt so *empty*. This triggered grief over my abandonment wound from childhood—I knew that I had not been abandoned by him, but it felt similar. By this time I had learned about emotional triggers and understood what was happening to me, so I shared my grief with Bill and received the comfort I needed, which enabled me to support David's independence and enjoy him when he returned home for breaks from school.

While writing this book, I had another grief trigger. Bill and I were on a plane, traveling for ministry in Arizona near where I grew up. We had just taken off when I looked out the window and could see my mom's house that we had just sold. I teared up as I explained to Bill, "I'll never be with her in that house again." A flood of grief memories came back to me, including the emotionally difficult days right before she died. I was caring for her, but she was not able to respond to me or interact with me, even though she did perk up whenever a friend visited her. I felt unappreciated. I knew it was her body shutting down and nearing death, but it was a familiar emotional wound. That triggered my past grief and abandonment.

We can have positive emotional triggers too. For example, when our plane landed in Arizona, I had feelings of gratitude for all the good I experienced when I lived there.

Calming emotional triggers is challenging, especially if we misinterpret Scripture in ways that undermine emotional and spiritual healing. Social media feeds and even some sermons and podcasts often feature simplistic advice that is replete with biblical misinterpretations related to emotional traumas. Here are a few examples:

Biblical Misinterpretations About Emotional Trauma

"No harm will overtake you" (Ps. 91:10) is misused to expect God to protect you from all pain.

The Lord "heals the brokenhearted" (Ps. 147:3) is misused to discount that emotional healing is usually a process.

"In all things God works for the good" (Rom. 8:28) is misused to minimize trauma and trials.

To "suffer according to God's will" (1 Pet. 4:19) is misused to believe God causes suffering.

Along these same lines, probably you've been told, "Change your thinking to change your feelings." Usually that strategy is insufficient and sometimes it is shaming, especially for trauma and other emotional wounds.

Your emotions are not problems to be fixed—they are expressions of your inner self that need to be known and loved. The Bible's path to peace, joy, and boldness starts with empathy, not rationalizing your emotions to wipe them away. Wise and healthy thinking integrates with feelings and relational connections.

Job in the Old Testament suffered from unrelenting trauma, with each new pain and grief triggering the previous wounds. Through thirty-six of the book's forty-two chapters Job vents his misery and fury, and his faith in God starts to falter as his depression deepens. But his friends keep giving him "proverbs of ashes," not empathy and prayer. When God manifests in a whirlwind at the end of the book, many Bible readers misinterpret it as God angrily judging Job. All along God had been listening to Job's complaints with empathy, and then in the whirlwind the Lord spoke to correct Job's friends, who had been giving him unfeeling and smug advice rather than empathy, and to affirm Job's great faith (Job 42:7–9). As is often true for us, *in his trauma Job had trouble finding God, but God found Job and blessed him greatly.*

The Cycle of Emotional Triggers

Getting emotionally triggered is part of a cycle that may keep repeating in ways that are painful and disruptive. When I was a little girl, my dad took me with him on a drive to see some houses burning down from a fire in our city. It scared me to see red flames leaping up to swallow a family's house. I felt for them as if it was my house. My father did not mean to scare me. He thought I didn't need to be afraid because I was safe with him. But all through my childhood I was afraid of fires, even fireworks. My family didn't understand it was an emotional trigger when they tried to get me to enjoy fireworks shows.

Not long after the house fire incident, I was at church when a huge thunderstorm struck. I became so scared that the lightning would start a fire that I left my friends and the fun activity we were doing and made a beeline to our car. I had heard that to be safe from lightning you needed to have rubber between you and the ground, so I ran to our car, hid in the back seat, and curled up into a fetal position. I covered my ears, but still every thunderbolt was so loud that it hurt my eardrums, crashed inside me, and made my whole body shake. I couldn't stop trembling. In my mind I could hear my parents telling me, *Snap out of it, Kristi! The thunder won't hurt you.* I was so afraid and embarrassed for anyone to see me feeling afraid.

My experience as a child who was emotionally triggered by lightning and thunder illustrates what we've identified as the Cycle of Emotional Triggers.

Cycle of Emotional Triggers

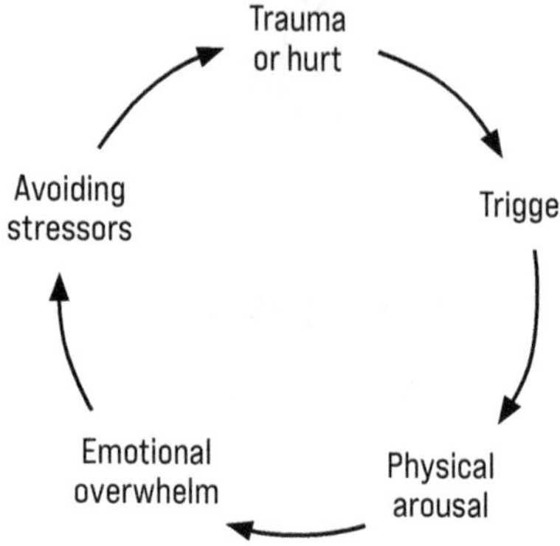

Trauma or Hurt

Experiencing a trauma, grief, or other emotional wound is likely to embed in our bodies and imprint in our sensitive souls, becoming like a land mine buried in a field.

Trigger

Current events that remind us of a past trauma, hurt, or other stressor can cause us to reexperience the past event.

Physical Arousal

Experiencing an intense emotional trigger is like stepping on a buried land mine. Without warning, our body explodes with distressing symptoms like flashbacks, sudden weeping, surging adrenaline, a racing heart, shortness of breath, physical shaking, muscle tension, or digestive problems.

Emotional Overwhelm

Then we are likely to become conscious of our emotions and perhaps flooded with emotions. We may feel fear, vulnerability, helplessness, grief, anger, anxiety, shame, or loneliness.

Avoiding Stressors

If you've experienced an overpowering trigger, it's natural to try to avoid it in the future. We may not even realize that we've developed coping mechanisms like overeating, overworking, drinking alcohol, using porn, or isolating to prevent remembering and reexperiencing a trauma or emotional wound.

As you can see, when past traumas and hurts get triggered, they reverberate in your embodied soul. Trauma and emotional wounds tend to self-perpetuate if they're not comforted and healed. They may cause anxiety, panic attacks, PTSD, depression, addiction, relational conflicts, illness, or distrust in God. As an adult, violations and emotional upsets may take you back in time so that you feel what you felt at that younger age, take on that immature identity, and regress to the insecure attachment you had then. For instance, after denying that he even knew Jesus and experiencing the trauma of seeing his Messiah and Lord crucified, the apostle Peter reverted to his old self from before he knew Jesus. He collapsed in shame, believed that he could never be a rock for Jesus, and went back to fishing. Similarly, when the Israelites were stuck in the desert wilderness for so many years, they wanted to go back to Egypt—they regressed to their previous identity as slaves and no longer believed that they were heirs of the promised land.

Calming Your Emotional Triggers

While Kristi and I (Bill) were on vacation in Austria, we heard an old legend that illustrates the power of empathy for emotional trauma. In the twelfth century, Richard Lionheart, the king of England, was captured by the Austrian Duke Leopold and imprisoned in a secret location. Blondel, the king's faithful troubadour, was deeply concerned and looked everywhere for him. He traveled from one castle to the next, stood outside, and sang a song that only Lionheart would know, but he kept striking out—he could not find him. With undying love for his suffering king, he refused to give up and continued traveling to castle after castle and singing their song. Finally, outside a castle in Austria, Blondel sang and heard Lionheart sing back to him the next stanza of the song! They sang back and forth in resonance with their mirror neurons of empathy firing joyfully. Then England paid a ransom to get their king back.

When my (Kristi's) abandonment wound was triggered after visiting baby Grace in the ICU, it was like I got locked up in a dark prison. I had believed Satan's lie that whispered, *You were born with a terminal defect. Even though you survived, you're not a miracle. You're too emotional and needy. You're a burden.* I got pulled down into shame and depression and just wanted to hide. I felt like I had a plague, and I was afraid that others would get sick if I opened my mouth to speak. But Bill saw me buried in shame. He drew out my emotions and listened to me with a gentle heart, patience, and love. Finally, I came up for air. I trusted the Lord's empathy—it was like Jesus was holding me.

The next morning I spontaneously remembered my grandma's face shining over me as a girl as she exclaimed, "Kristi, you're a miracle! God has a special purpose for your life! Don't you ever forget it."

Through receiving empathy, I heard Jesus' love song and was released from my prison of shame and isolation and was able to self-regulate and calm my emotions. The little girl in me who had felt alone and unwanted was walking free in the sunlight of God's heartwarming love. I could see and trust the Lord's shining face of love in my grandma telling me that I was a miracle. Then Bible promises started to click in for me at a heart level, like these:

"Those who look to [the Lord] are radiant; their faces are never covered with shame" (Ps. 34:5).

The Lord says, "I have chosen you and have not rejected you. So do not fear, for I am with you" (Isa. 41:9–10).

"Nothing . . . will ever be able to separate us from the love of God that is revealed in Christ Jesus our Lord" (Rom. 8:39 NLT).

"God has said, 'Never will I leave you; never will I forsake you'" (Heb. 13:5).

My personal history with trauma and emotional triggers has come full circle. For many years I've been honored to care for others with these struggles and help them receive the Lord's empathy and strength. I've learned it's important for us to establish some simple soul care practices that we can immediately engage when we get emotionally triggered or distressed. I encourage you to try a few of these tips for grounding yourself emotionally by receiving God's comfort and strength in the present moment:

- Ask for empathy from a safe person.
- Ride the wave of emotion (don't try to control it).
- Recall and appreciate a time you felt cared for.
- Recite comforting Scriptures.
- Listen to music you enjoy.
- Savor your favorite tea or coffee.
- Journal a prayer about your experience.
- Take a prayer walk and notice nature.

As you saw in my story above, receiving Jesus' empathy through Bill, recalling my grandma's care, and reciting comforting Scriptures were three emotionally grounding practices that calmed my trauma trigger. These are ways I practiced self-empathy by agreeing with God's grace for me.

Four A's of Empathy for Emotional Triggers

Practicing the Four A's of Empathy can help you to regulate your emotions when you've been triggered or are distressed. You can apply these steps to a past emotional trigger or one you're currently struggling with. You can also apply them to give empathy to a friend who is emotionally triggered.

1. **Ask** questions

   What happened to trigger me?

   What does this remind me of in the past?

   How is this trigger affecting my body and physical activity?

   What emotions am I feeling?

2. **Attune** to emotions

   I feel flooded emotionally.

   It scared me when _______ happened.

   I feel shame about ________.

   I'm sad because ________.

   I feel grateful for ________.

3. **Acknowledge** the significance

   This is overwhelming because I need __________.

   The timing is hard because I was already stressed (or hurting) over __________.

This is discouraging—I thought I had gotten over this trauma.

It's especially difficult because this trigger reminds me of __________.

4. **Affirm** strengths

I'm recognizing that trying to deny or avoid my emotions about this issue is not helping me.

I've taken a good and healthy step to articulate the emotions that got triggered for me.

I'm thankful that the Lord Jesus is calming my trigger and the emotions it stirred up and is giving me strength to move forward.

EMPATHY PRACTICE:

Calming Touch Prayer

Sometimes when I (Bill) feel overwhelmed, stressed, or tired, Kristi gently strokes my face with her fingers and prays silently for me. As she does this, I receive her loving touches as a gift of grace and offer silent prayers of thanks for God's empathy and comfort. (I also enjoy offering this blessing to Kristi.) We call this Calming Touch Prayer.

When you experience trauma or any stressor, it can get internalized and stored in your body. It's important to get help with releasing the pain and distress and internalizing God's comfort and peace. Calming Touch Prayer is a way to do this and it can be self-administered. The power of soothing touch from a loved one or your own self has been validated in psychological studies. It stimulates oxytocin, the body's natural hormone that produces feelings of love, warmth, and comfort.[4] It also reduces the body's production of the stress hormone cortisol.[5]

Jesus' touch meant so much to the children he blessed (Mark 10:13–16) and the people he healed, like the lepers that no one but him dared to touch (Matt. 8:2–3). Soothing touch can be a powerful expression of comfort, but ultimately it's a *spiritual touch* from Holy Spirit that connects us with God's love and healing power. Like the woman with the blood disorder, we can touch Jesus with our *faith* (Mark 5:25–34). When you are emotionally triggered or in any situation of need, Calming Touch Prayer can help you know and feel that you are deeply loved by your Lord and Healer.

Calming Touch Prayer Steps

These steps can help you receive God's comfort when you're experiencing emotional distress or a trigger. Add in each step till you're doing all three at the same time. You can do Calming Touch Prayer for self-soothing or for loved ones to take turns soothing each other.

1. *Give calming touch.* Use your fingers in a circular motion to softly caress the forehead, eyebrows, soft tissue under the eyes, and cheeks. You can also gently stroke the head, neck, shoulders, or feet.
2. *Visualize Jesus.* Imagine Jesus touching you to minister his soothing comfort as he did in the Gospels for someone he healed or a child he blessed.
3. *Pray with thankfulness.* Give thanks to Jesus Christ for his empathy, comfort, and healing touch.

More Ways to Self-Soothe

Place your arms across your chest and use your hands to stroke your arms up and down.

Flatten your hands and press them together, like praying hands, and then rub them up and down.

SOUL TALK

1. What did you learn about trauma and emotional triggers?
2. How do you (or a loved one) relate to experiencing emotional triggers from past hurts, trauma, or grief?
3. What is a favorite Bible promise that has "clicked in" at a heart level for you?
4. Which of the Four A's of Empathy for emotional triggers seems most helpful for you to work on?
5. What was your experience with using Calming Touch Prayer as a method to receive God's empathy and comfort?

9

Governing Anger with Love

In your anger do not sin.

Ephesians 4:26

It's natural to get angry if you are being mistreated by someone, are frustrated about something that went wrong, or feel like someone has become an enemy. At these times it may seem like no one is on your side. When you feel vulnerable, anger can amp you up to make you feel powerful. Part of you may want to let loose with your anger! But you don't really want to hurt anyone, because someone's anger has hurt you in the past and you don't want to do that to anyone else. *Whether you react in anger or hold it in, it's stressful and tiring to manage anger.*

Jesus and the people he loved were sinned against, abused, disrespected, rejected, and hurt in many ways. Our Lord felt angry at times like these, especially when the offenses came from religious leaders who had been entrusted by God to shepherd the people with mercy, wisdom, and love. He was tempted to sin in every way that we are, including with anger (Heb. 4:15). Yet he always governed his anger with love. When you are angry, Jesus does not condemn you—he feels for you with empathy and appreciates that you seek to love people and not hurt them with anger.

> *Lord Jesus, you are a trustworthy judge because in you truth and grace kiss. Thank you that you always govern your anger with loving-kindness for me and others.*

"He Makes Me Angry!"

Ricky fumed, "He makes me so mad!" I (Bill) was thankful to hear this. It was a breakthrough for him to let his anger rip. He had been mistreated by his boss, who had put him on a forced leave of absence and stripped him of his longtime leadership role. For two months he had been depressed and soft-pedaling his anger in his therapy sessions with me. I kept giving him more rope to be angry and prodded him to be gut honest with me.

Finally Ricky was letting loose. He continued, "It's not fair. He had a secret board meeting without me and rallied everyone against me. He didn't even talk to me about it—he just told me. He says a couple of people were intimidated by me and so I had to find another job. He won't let me talk to anyone about it. All my employee reviews have been A+. I helped him build this organization from the ground up. He's spineless!"

Ricky saw I could handle his anger at full throttle and had empathy for him. Later, I helped him work through the intertwining processes of grieving what he'd lost and forgiving how he'd been wronged by his boss and board members.

I imagine at times we all have protested, "He (or she) makes me angry!" There is a wide range of issues that can throw us off-kilter and evoke angry reactions, from smaller irritations like calling your insurance company and being put on hold for an hour to larger offenses like being betrayed by a loved one you trusted.

Sometimes we get angry at our own selves. Recently, a baseball player for the Chicago Cubs was so angry about his poor pitching performance that he punched a wall and broke his hand, which put him on the injury list for the rest of the season.[1] It's easy to see that was not smart, but I imagine we all punch ourselves with self-criticism at times, saying negative things about ourselves to ourselves. Turning against yourself with anger can break your soul and leave you suffering in shame.

We may not want to admit it, but at times we even get angry at God. You don't have to feel guilty and alone if you are angry at God. As we've seen, the Bible is a real and raw book, showing us situations where God's people express anger, including at God.

Bible Characters Who Got Angry

Job and his wife railed in anger at God when he let them suffer so much (Job 2:9; 19:6–7).

Naomi was bitterly angry at God when her husband and sons died (Ruth 1:20–21).

David was angry at God for abandoning him (words that Jesus recited; Ps. 22:1).

The psalmist accused God of going to sleep and not protecting his people (Ps. 44:23–24).

Jonah fumed at God for showing mercy to his enemies (Jon. 4:1).

Martha protested to Jesus for not coming sooner to heal her brother (John 11:21).

Paul and Barnabas had a sharp argument and parted company (Acts 15:39).

Examples like these give us empathy, grace, and guidance when we feel angry at God.

Understanding Anger

Even though it may feel like someone *makes* you angry, the truth is that no one "makes" you angry. When you are angry it's your responsibility. It's your anger, so it's mostly about you—not someone else or the situation. It's about your emotions, your attitude, your needs, and your reactions. Blaming other people for our anger keeps us stuck in it and poisoned by resentment.

Anger is a feeling of being wronged. It's a God-given emotion that's natural. It's appropriate to feel angry if your boundaries are crossed, you are mistreated, or you don't get what you need or what is fair and just. It's also appropriate to feel angry because you need to protect other people who have been wronged.

Anger is also an *energy* that moves your will to right what is wrong—or what you perceive to be wrong. In this sense anger is *directional* and gets aimed at another person, your own self, or a situation. That's dangerous. When anger is poorly aimed, someone gets hurt. In fact, even if anger is rightly aimed or includes helpful feedback, it's likely to feel hurtful to people. This is why it's important to speak the truth *in love* (Eph. 4:15).

Another danger with anger is that it tends to combine with self-righteousness because we feel like we've been mistreated (or someone we care about has been mistreated), and our anger activates us to rise up and right the wrong. Self-righteous anger is prideful and rashly judges others rather than submitting the situation to God to be the righteous and loving judge. It overestimates our own abilities to measure out justice. It's likely to be hurtful and harmful to other people and our own self. Scripture teaches us, "Don't hit back; discover beauty in everyone. If you've got it in you, get along with everybody. Don't insist on getting even; that's not for you to do. 'I'll do the judging,' says God. 'I'll take care of it'" (Rom. 12:17–19 MSG).

Self-righteous anger neglects the humble and wise work of examining ourselves, trusting God, forgiving others, and having empathy for those we feel wronged by. That's why Jesus gave us this clear and direct teaching: "Do not judge, or you too will be judged. For in the same way you judge others, you will be judged, and with the measure you use, it will be measured to you" (Matt. 7:1-2).

Healthy anger is like an alarm to wake us up to a problem or injury that needs to be dealt with. That's why Paul teaches in Ephesians 4, "'In your anger do not sin': Do not let the sun go down while you are still angry" (v. 26). He's not telling us to "be angry" as if we could just get it out and be done with it. Nor does he make the opposite mistake of judging and shaming us for having angry emotions. Instead, he warns us that holding on to anger is damaging. It gives the devil a foothold and grieves Holy Spirit (vv. 27, 30). Repressed anger leads to bitterness, angry outbursts, angry conflicts, slander, and malice (v. 31). In contrast, healthy anger goes with mutual relationships marked by speaking the truth with love, kindness, compassion, and forgiveness, as Christ does with us (vv. 15, 25, 32).

Benefits of Healthy Anger

Harnesses your pent-up energy for being assertive.

Works to solve your problems and reverse injustice.

Strengthens your boundaries of safety and protection.

Relieves your shame or depression (anger against yourself).

Increases your emotional intelligence.

Supports you giving and receiving deeper forgiveness.

Anger Assessment

Anger is probably the emotion that is the hardest to manage. Most of us at times have harmed others or ourselves with our anger. In one survey, 64 percent of people said they had experienced office rage and 45 percent admitted they regularly lose their temper at work.[2] In another survey, 28 percent of people reported that they worry about how angry they sometimes feel.[3] Our Anger Assessment will give you insights into any tendencies you have to react to anger or internalize it.

Answer each question below as *mostly true* (T) or *mostly false* (F). Mostly true means "Often I experience this."

1. In conflicts I raise my voice in anger without realizing it. T F
2. I hold my anger inside and get depressed. T F
3. I get into angry arguments on issues that shouldn't be such a big deal. T F
4. When I'm angry at someone it leaks out to other people with criticism. T F
5. When I get angry I say or do things that I regret. T F
6. I try to please people to avoid conflicts and keep the peace. T F
7. If someone is angry at me, I get angry at them. T F

8. When I feel upset at someone I avoid them. T F
9. When I get angry I yell, hit something, or break something. T F
10. I don't like being angry with other people. T F
11. I like to argue because I can get at the truth. T F
12. When I'm angry I feel guilty or afraid I'll hurt someone. T F
13. When I'm angry I tend to say mean things. T F
14. When someone offends me I stew in anger for a long time. T F
15. People tell me they feel criticized or judged by me. T F

The odd-numbered questions refer to having angry reactions (often toward other people) and the even-numbered questions refer to internalizing anger. If you responded "mostly true" to six or more examples of struggling with anger, consider talking with a Soul Shepherding spiritual director or coach who can give you empathy, insight, and prayer. Visit SoulShepherding.org/DeeplyLoved or scan this QR code.

The Psychology of Anger

Bill and I (Kristi) were speaking at a church and Ashley asked, "I went to therapy and got in touch with my emotions, but I don't think it was a good thing, because now I feel angry most of the time. It seems I functioned better without negative emotions.

It feels uncomfortable, horrible actually—I don't want to get angry at my husband and people I love. What's going on with me?"

I explained that in a journey of healing and growth often we feel worse before we feel better. In her case, speaking about her needs and disagreements made her feel guilty because it created conflict with people who wanted her to be agreeable all the time, like she used to be. But taking courage to express her true self was important for her well-being and relationships. She agreed and admitted, "Since feeling my anger and being more honest, I have been less anxious and depressed than before."

When Ashley was a child, she was hurt by anger and recurring conflicts in her family. She did not receive empathy or guidance on how to deal with emotions like anger in a healthy way or how to communicate effectively and graciously to resolve conflicts. She had latched on to some confusing and damaging misinterpretations of God's Word related to anger.

Biblical Misinterpretations About Anger

"Refrain from anger" (Ps. 37:8) is misused to judge anger as bad and deny it.

"Turn . . . the other cheek" (Matt. 5:39) is misused to reject healthy assertiveness.

"Live at peace with everyone" (Rom. 12:18) is misused to avoid conflict resolution.

"Be angry" (Eph. 4:26 ESV) is misused to justify all anger as righteous (opposite from the first one above).

Anger is like fire—it's powerful and can be used constructively or destructively. Fire can be used to cook food, heat a cold house, and generate electricity, but it also can burn down a forest and kill someone. Similarly, anger can help you set boundaries and be assertive to speak the truth in love, but it also can lead you to violate another person or have a heart attack.

We read an article in *The New York Times* that illustrates destructive anger spreading like wildfire as anger begets more anger and the pain and injustice escalate. An auto shop employee abruptly quit his job and requested his final paycheck of $915 in wages owed. The boss was mad over being left in the lurch and dragged his feet on payment. The former employee kept demanding payment, so finally the boss got revenge by dumping 91,500 greasy pennies on his driveway! The former employee then upped the ante to get his own revenge by posting the company's injustice on Instagram. Finally, the US Department of Labor got involved, determined that the fault lay with the employer, and filed a lawsuit against his company for retaliation.[4]

Cycle of Anger

Anger is a complex emotion. Often it functions as a secondary emotion that is a reaction to other emotions. In fact, one study identified nineteen emotions that may be hiding under anger, including hurt, sadness, fear, anxiety, guilt, shame, grief, loneliness, jealousy, and confusion.[5] But other times anger is the emotion that's hiding behind other emotions. The Cycle of Anger diagram on the next page helps you understand how anger tends to relate to other emotions as well as to stress, attitude, and hormones.

Cycle of Anger

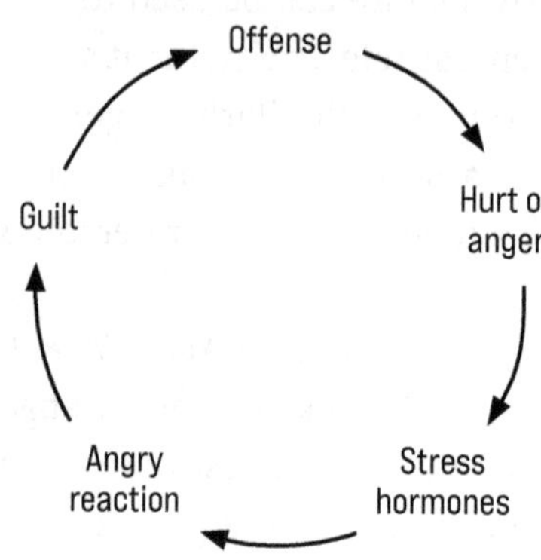

Offense

When someone crosses your boundaries, thwarts your will, or mistreats you, it's an offense that initiates the Cycle of Anger. Even if you perceive that you've been offended when you were not, it will still initiate this cycle.

Hurt or Anger

When you are mistreated it's natural to feel hurt in some way. Hurts make us feel vulnerable, so sometimes they hide under anger. It's also natural to feel angry when you're mistreated, but anger often hides under hurt, anxiety, or shame. When emotional distress is denied, it remains in your body and will be rekindled by future offenses. This is why you may have one hundred volts of anger in a situation that only calls for ten volts.

Stress Hormones

When anger heats up in your body, whether it's boiling in rage or simmering in resentment, it activates stress hormones of cortisol and adrenaline, your heart rate increases, your muscles tense up, and you might get a headache or grind your teeth.

Angry Reaction

Hot anger in your body is likely to eventually erupt like a volcano with angry words or actions, or it may steam out in irritability, negative comments, slander, sarcasm, withdrawal, stubbornness, contempt, or passive-aggressive behavior.

Guilt

Angry outbursts and other expressions of anger are likely to cause guilt and shame, which can add fuel to repeat the Cycle of Anger. Or the pain of guilt can motivate you to exit the cycle by seeking empathy, shifting from self-condemnation to sadness, and learning how to govern anger with love.

Anger That's Off Base

Often our anger gets off base when we inaccurately perceive a situation. Brennan Manning tells the story of a famous author who was riding the subway in New York City while quietly reading a book. At one stop a man and his children blasted onto the train. The children were wildly running about, messing around, and making a commotion. The kids were so noisy and distracting that the author couldn't read his book. Finally, he turned to the father and complained, "Sir, perhaps you could restore order here by telling your children to sit down." The man replied with a downcast face, "I know I should do something. We just came from the hospital. Their mother died an hour ago. I just don't know what to do."[6]

The author misjudged the father based on a wrong assumption. When we are angry at someone there's always *one more fact* that would help us understand and have empathy for that person. The point is not to deny your angry feelings or shame yourself—that is not loving for you or others. The point is to be careful with how you express your anger, because when you're angry it usually will feel self-righteous and tempt you to be the judge. Jesus says, "Do not judge, or you too will be judged" (Matt. 7:1). Instead of putting ourselves in the superior position by judging someone else, we need to discard our measuring rod for other people, cultivate an uncritical temper, and entrust judgment to God. Our sovereign Lord is the eternal judge and the only one who is capable and trustworthy to balance justice and mercy for others and our own selves (Rom. 2:1–4). This is another vantage point on why the first thing to do when you feel angry is to seek empathy, which can help give you better perspective.

One time I (Bill) was driving in traffic on a congested freeway. I had been practicing being unhurried, so I was listening to classical music as I drove in the slow lane and stayed a few generous car lengths behind the car ahead of me. Suddenly, a car that had been right behind me swerved out to the left, raced by, swerved in front of me, and slowed down. Immediately, I had to slow down. White-knuckling the steering wheel, I fumed. *How rude! He makes me so angry! Doesn't he have any consideration for other people?* I wanted to ram into his bumper! A minute later he rocketed out of sight.

Many people feel angry when they're driving their car. I know because when I'm speaking and tell this story, audience members respond with guilty chuckles or elbow their spouse! But that's not the reason I tell the story; the reason is for us to resist angrily judging other people and seek help for our own anger. Whatever situation you find yourself in—including when you're angry—see it as Jesus' school of discipleship for you.

In my car, after I caught my breath and loosened my grip on the steering wheel, I tuned in to my emotions with self-empathy: *Why does this make me angry? I was scared of getting hurt. Additionally, I have a chip on my shoulder about rudeness. I try hard to never be inconsiderate of others because in my life that's been so hurtful to me. When someone is rude or inconsiderate to me it evokes repressed anger.* My angry reaction was not just about the driver being reckless, it was also about my pent-up anger. We often get angry when we unconsciously encounter our shadow self in another person. The shadow self is made up of the parts of ourselves that we don't like and try to deny. It's unconscious and we readily project it onto other people and judge them for it. Instead, we need to take responsibility for our anger.

Using the imagery of the log and speck in Matthew 7:3–5, Jesus explained about the dangers of projecting our own issues onto others and judging them:

> Don't condemn people or you will be condemned. Why are you bothered with the speck of sawdust in your neighbor's eye when *you have a log of condemnation in your own eye*? Get to work on your own log! You'll get specks in your own eyes and then you'll understand and be more compassionate toward other people's pain. (author's paraphrase)[7]

Once I had named my anger and understood its source, then I was able to connect with Jesus' empathy for me and verbalize it for myself: *I can relax. Jesus is with me and he cares for me. I'm deeply loved and safe.* Then I prayed for the reckless driver: *Lord Jesus, I ask you to help this man drive safely so no one gets hurt. He's stressed and rushed today; please care for him. Amen.* Jesus' empathetic love for me and this man calmed my anger. I became peaceful and happy. I enjoyed partnering with Jesus to bless the one who had "cursed" me by endangering me (see Luke 6:28).

Emotional Intelligence and Anger

Some time ago, I (Bill) was tired from back-to-back ministry trips and recovering from sickness. I was on a phone call with someone on our staff about a difficult project, and I got impatient and frustrated. Afterward, I was stewing in agitation. I was also afraid that my anger had leaked out and was hurtful. I started to judge myself till my spirit was drooping in shame. Condemning thoughts swarmed me like killer bees: *What's the matter with you? You afflicted her with your perfectionism, negativity, and anger. You're not living your teachings. You're a bad leader!*

Then I told Kristi what happened and poured out my heart. She threw me a lifeline with multiple heartfelt expressions of empathy and a couple of gracious affirmations at the end. I felt myself in a spiritual tussle. Holy Spirit was touching my heart softly in love, but a rancorous spirit was trying to pull me back down. I felt self-pity, and part of me actually wanted to just give in and stay depressed and frustrated. But I grabbed hold of Jesus' lifeline of empathy through Kristi. I agreed with her posture toward me, becoming nonjudgmental and accepting of my stressed and angry emotions. In other words, I developed self-empathy. Then I talked to my teammate to apologize and give her empathy. She appreciated the empathy and gave me empathy as well. God brought repair and redemption.

In the midst of that storm of anger and shame I did not feel like I was exercising emotional intelligence (EQ), but actually I was. I paid attention to my feelings of anger like a red light on the dashboard of my soul and received God's empathy through Kristi. I was able to access the five traits of being emotionally SMART:[8]

Self-awareness: Receiving empathy helped me understand and accept my emotions.

Managing emotions: I was able to soothe my shame and calm my anger.

Activation: I was motivated to care for myself and my teammate.

Relating with empathy: I showed concern for my teammate's emotions and listened to her.

Teaming with others: We repaired our conflict and resumed working on the project.

I've learned that when someone might feel hurt by me it's important to go back and apologize, but that is not sufficient to repair the relationship. It's also important to give empathy by asking questions, listening, and offering a tender heart to understand and care. For instance, you can ask, "How did that feel for you? . . . What else did you experience? . . . What do you need from me now?"

Research studies have validated that increasing your EQ helps diminish aggressive anger.[9] The key to improving your EQ in your work and relationships is receiving empathy that fosters awareness and acceptance of your emotions, supports you with managing your emotions, and cultivates your empathy for others.

Four A's of Empathy for Anger

Receiving empathy helps us cultivate emotional intelligence and govern anger with love. You can use the following empathy prompts for self-empathy or giving empathy to others.

1. **Ask** QUESTIONS

   What am I angry about?

   When have I been angry about a similar situation?

   What might God be teaching me about why I get angry and what I need?

2. **ATTUNE** TO EMOTIONS

   I'm irritable because I don't like it when people ______.

   I'm angry because I feel hurt . . . scared . . . my needs weren't met . . .

3. **ACKNOWLEDGE** THE SIGNIFICANCE

   This is a big deal for me because he crossed my boundary.

   That incident turned up the heat on my anger that was already boiling.

   Reacting with anger has hurt me by causing ______.

   I got angry about this because my need for ______ was disrespected.

4. **AFFIRM** STRENGTHS

   Jesus, I'm thankful that your love for me and this person is stronger than my anger . . . It's encouraging that God is teaching me to feel my anger and not react to it . . .

EMPATHY PRACTICE:

Praying an Angry Psalm

When I (Bill) have felt betrayed or sinned against in another way, Psalm 35 is one of the angry psalms that helps me to pray.[10] In this psalm David is angry at friends who have turned against him, falsely accused him, plotted his downfall, and knifed him in the back. When you experience injustices or offenses like these, it's good to make David's prayer your own. Praying Psalm 35 helps you to:

- Name your anger and related emotions.
- Take courage and be vulnerable in prayer.
- Receive empathy and validation from God.
- Let go of control and release the results to God.
- Not feel judged or isolated for being angry.

Psalm 35

Harass these hecklers, God,
  punch these bullies in the nose. . . .
When those thugs try to knife me in the back,
  make them look foolish. . . .

But let me run loose and free,
    celebrating God's great work . . .
Do what you think is right, God, my God,
    but don't make me pay for their good time. . . .
But those who want
    the best for me,
Let them have the last word—a glad shout!—
    and say, over and over and over,
"God is great—everything works
    together for good for his servant."
I'll tell the world how great and good you are,
    I'll shout Hallelujah all day, every day.

(Ps. 35:1, 4, 9, 24, 27–28 MSG)

Prayer Prompts

1. Express your anger.

   "Harass these hecklers, God . . ." Rely on God's empathy by telling him concretely how you've been harassed or mistreated and expressing your angry feelings.

2. Ask for what you need.

   "But let me run loose and free . . ." Ask God for what you want and need.

3. Abandon outcomes to God.

   "Do what you think is right, God, my God . . ." Offer a prayer abandoning the outcomes of your situation to the sovereign Lord.

4. Give thanks for your friends.

   "But those who want the best for me . . ." Give thanks to God for your friend(s), for their empathy, and for "the best" things that they want for you.

5. Praise God for his good works.

   "God is great—everything works together for good for his servant . . ." Give praise to God for his greatness and the good he is bringing to you. Then pray blessings for your enemy.

SOUL TALK

1. What did you learn about anger?
2. Which biblical misinterpretation of anger has impacted you?
3. When you were a child, what was your experience with anger in your family?
4. What can you work on to improve your emotional intelligence to help you govern your anger with love?
5. Which of the five aspects of praying Psalm 35 are especially helpful to you? Why?

10

Caring for Others Without Getting Drained

> Offer each other a helping hand. . . . We each must carry our own load.
>
> Galatians 6:2, 5 CEV

Perhaps you have been giving and giving and giving and need to slow down and breathe. Bill and I (Kristi) have felt that way at times. We've sat at the computer and been wordless when we needed to reply to a request or give care and prayer for someone who is hurting. We've felt too weary to pick up the phone and bless a loved one who needed it. We've felt drained from caring for others.

Even Jesus felt power go out from him when the woman touched his garment in faith (Mark 5:30). At times after intensive ministry, it seems he felt empathy fatigue and needed to withdraw to get some breathing space and pray (Matt. 14:13;

Mark 1:35; Luke 5:16). None of us can live on exhales—we need to inhale and then exhale. Your soul needs the nourishment of empathy. You've been caring for people and serving God, and now it's your turn. *Jesus sees you and smiles*. He appreciates each time you've listened or offered a helping hand to someone. He has empathy for you and wants to help you care for your soul.

Jesus, you are the Lord and Savior and yet you show us that you have human needs. Thank you for nourishing our souls so we can care for others in your name without getting drained.

What Weights Are You Carrying?

I (Kristi) was about to travel to lead one of our Soul Shepherding Institute retreats. I picked up my backpack and thought, *Wow! How did that get so heavy? What did I put in my backpack?* I opened it up and saw my computer, charging cords, Bible, retreat notebook, water bottle, and lunch. I was surprised that those things added up to so much weight. Identifying what was in my backpack and knowing I needed each item made it easier to carry. Assessing how heavy it was helped me adjust my expectations for myself. I wouldn't be able to carry the heavy weight as far as I wanted and would need to lift it off my shoulders more often in order to rest. Still, my neck and shoulders were sore at the end of the day. I massaged my aching muscles and adjusted my plans for exercise the next morning. I gave my body time to recover and that allowed me to get my strength back.

In your daily life, each person you care for adds weight to your backpack. It gets too heavy to carry when lots of people need your care, especially if some of them are not taking responsibility for themselves or you are trying too hard to help them.

When Empathy Is Draining

Over the years we've journeyed with many people who had empathy fatigue or compassion fatigue. You may relate.

A woman was babysitting her granddaughter three days a week so her daughter could work, she was talking with her sister every day to help her recover from a divorce, she was praying for her son in college who was deconstructing his faith, and her father was leaning heavily on her for support since her mother got dementia. She thought her weariness was because she had not been doing enough spiritual disciplines, especially solitude. Her empathy was draining her because she was overextending herself.

A man's younger brother had lost his job after getting drunk again. The man gave his car to his brother "to help him get back on his feet." His wife protested, "I'm tired of being used by him. We've paid for detox, rent, attorney fees—when does it end?" She resented being roped into doing more and more to rescue her brother-in-law.

"If I let myself feel my emotions and receive empathy," a surgeon insisted, "then I won't be able to do my job. I have to be clearheaded and ready to make quick decisions that can help save someone's life." But in her personal life she did not know how to make space for her emotions or how to care for her soul. She was burned out.

Day and night and even on weekends people wanted their pastor's care. "How can I say no? I'm the only person they trust when they're hurting, sick, or need prayer."

A woman on retreat with us admitted, "I am so depleted from mothering and teaching children in the classroom that I have no words." Since she had no words, she went through a crayon box. She found herself picking out all the broken crayons and realized *she* felt like a broken crayon. Then she drew a picture of herself collapsed on the ground in front of a wall.

In each of these examples, the person was getting drained by their empathy for others. In different ways they were caught in codependent patterns of enmeshing with people they cared for and overfunctioning to help them. They were lacking healthy boundaries of self-differentiation and self-care.

Codependency Assessment

It's common for people to have some traits of codependency where they take too much responsibility for other people. One study found that 74 percent of nursing students reported codependency traits.[1] Another study of college students found that 85 percent of the males and 76 percent of the females were high in codependency traits (which reverses the gender stereotype).[2] Our Codependency Assessment will give you insights into how you approach your relationships.

Answer each question below as *mostly true* (T) or *mostly false* (F). Mostly true means, "Often I experience this."

1. I tolerate mistreatment from people in hopes of being loved. T F

2. I feel compelled to help people solve their problems. T F

3. I try to rescue others from the consequences of their irresponsible behavior. T F

4. If I'm not helping someone, I feel empty, bored, or unimportant. T F

5. It's hard for me to say no when someone asks for my help. T F

6. It's hard for me to ask others for help. T F
7. In close relationships I neglect to care for my own needs. T F
8. I'm quick to get angry about injustices done to others. T F
9. I tend to talk about other people and their problems. T F
10. I worry about how other people are feeling. T F
11. I worry about other people's opinions of me. T F
12. In potential conflicts with people I try to keep quiet. T F
13. It's hard for me to ask for what I want from a boss or authority figure. T F
14. I feel more comfortable giving to others rather than receiving. T F
15. It's difficult for me to receive empathy and care from others. T F

If you responded "mostly true" to six or more examples of struggling with codependency, consider talking with a Soul Shepherding spiritual director or coach who can listen to you with empathy, help you set healthier boundaries, and pray for you. Visit SoulShepherding.org/DeeplyLoved or scan this QR code.

The Psychology of Codependency

Spiritual formation begins with what we call *family formation.* As children growing up in our families of origin we were shaped or misshaped through our relationships with our parents, siblings, and other loved ones. These early relationships, along with our biology and choices, form our relational attachment style, trust in God, self-awareness, self-identity, boundaries, and capacity to love others. Because family life includes stress and every family (and every group) has some unhealthy and unloving patterns, each member of a family tends to fall into one or more dysfunctional family roles.

For instance, I (Bill) was the oldest in my family growing up and became a parentified child. I was rewarded when I carried responsibility for my four younger siblings and helped my parents around the house. Kristi was the youngest in her family and became a pleaser. She says she didn't like feeling needy and emotional, so she tried to feel empowered and safe by managing her mother's emotions and serving her.

Another dysfunctional family role is the enabler. Enablers are overly responsible and overly focused on helping family members who have problems. They become codependent with one or more dysfunctional family members, such as those who take on the roles of the addict, the scapegoat who rebels against family values and gets negative attention, or the identified patient who has special needs or emotional struggles.

Enablers are described as "caretakers" because they care for others, yet unconsciously they are trying to *take care* from them by being appreciated or identifying with the needs of those they help. In other words, they try to live vicariously through the people they help. Enablers struggle with a wounded or weak sense of self-identity. Their lack of self-differentiation undermines their capacity for self-empathy and setting boundaries to care for their own soul.

In my teens and twenties my codependent patterns were made worse by misunderstanding and misapplying some key Scriptures in ways I (Bill) later learned were common among Christians. Careful study of the Bible and Jesus-centered psychology helped me uncover my mistakes and guide others with empathy and truth.

Biblical Misinterpretations About Helping Others

"Give to the one who asks you" (Matt. 5:42) is misused to believe you can't say no to people.

"Deny yourself" (Matt. 16:24) is misused to neglect self-awareness and self-identity.

"God will meet all your needs" (Phil. 4:19) is misused to avoid asking for help from people.

"Seek peace and pursue it" (1 Pet. 3:11) is misused to promote people-pleasing.

Cycle of Codependency

In a codependent relationship there is an unhealthy attachment between a *giver* and a *taker*. The taker is often someone who is highly dysfunctional. The enabler becomes the giver in a codependent relationship and can get addicted to unhealthy patterns of helping others.

Givers are usually highly responsible, compassionate, and more focused on other people's needs than their own. Takers tend to be irresponsible and have problems with addiction and abusing or manipulating others. Givers feel sorry for takers and try to rescue them from the pain and mess they're in. They think, *I have so much and this person has so little and just needs some help from me to get on track.* But their sacrificial help goes into a bottomless hole. The reason is that the taker is not exercising personal responsibility for their problems; the giver is more motivated for the taker's well-being than the taker is. In the dysfunctional relational dynamics of codependency, the giver gets used, manipulated, and abused. To make matters worse, when the giver rescues the taker by fixing their problems, it enables the taker's ongoing irresponsible and destructive behavior because they don't learn their lessons. The help of codependent givers is often unhealthy, causing them to feel drained, discouraged, angry, and resentful.

Understanding the Cycle of Codependency can help you set better boundaries and cultivate healthy and loving relationships.

Cycle of Codependency

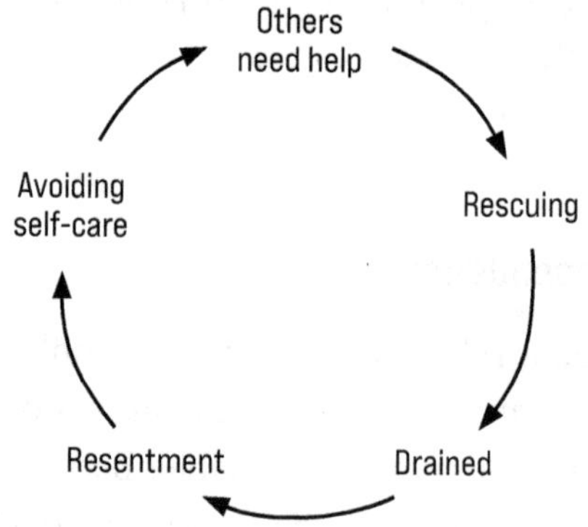

Others need help

Rescuing

Drained

Resentment

Avoiding self-care

Others Need Help

Giving and receiving help is natural and good, but in a codependent relationship the giver is *compelled* to help other people, including takers who are acting irresponsibly or stuck in unhealthy patterns.

Rescuing

A giver comes to rescue the taker. The theme of this dysfunctional dance is that the giver overfunctions and the taker underfunctions. Givers sacrifice themselves for the payback of feeling appreciated or powerful.

Drained

Givers get physically and emotionally exhausted if they deny their own emotions or if takers spoil their help. Givers who get stuck in the Cycle of Codependency are prone to empathy fatigue, anxiety, depression, sickness, and chronic fatigue.

Resentment

Because givers put other people's needs before their own, they build resentment. They need to get in touch with an inner angry protest that would say, "What about me? I'm giving so much here. What are you doing for me?" Healthy anger helps them set needed boundaries.

Avoiding Self-Care

Givers don't realize that they "need" to be needed by others to feel stimulated, affirmed, and distracted from their deep feelings of emptiness, insecurity, or shame. This is how codependency becomes an addiction. For givers to be healthy they need to take responsibility to ask for the empathy and care they need so they have the energy and capacity to care for others.

Codependency Is Not Empathy

A twelve-year-old boy kept the bottle-shaped cocoon of an emperor moth to watch its transformation from caterpillar to moth. Finally it began to push its way through the neck of the cocoon, but it seemed to get stuck. For days it squirmed and strived but made no headway. He resolved to give it a helping hand. With the tip of his scissors, he widened the opening a little bit and the moth was able to crawl out, dragging its swollen body and little wings. He was excited to see the moth finish its growth, spread its beautiful wings, and fly! But the moth soon shriveled and died. The boy's "misplaced tenderness" had ruined the moth. It needed the painful journey of pressing all the way through the narrow opening of the cocoon so that fluid would be forced into its wings till they grew enough that the moth would be ready to fly when it came out of the cocoon.[3]

That's the deception and destructiveness of codependency—it seems empathetic and loving but it gets off track. We think we are helping people who are stuck or struggling by rescuing them from painful trials, but it's misplaced tenderness. Those trials are designed by God to teach them important lessons like enduring hardship as loving discipline from their heavenly Father (Heb. 12:7–11).

Embedded in rescuing other people is a Messiah complex. Ironically, even Jesus the Messiah did not have a Messiah complex; he did not pridefully rush in to rescue people who did not want to change. For instance, after Jesus fed the crowd of five thousand with bread from heaven, they were excited and tried to make him their king who would overthrow the Romans and usher in a new golden age for Israel, but Jesus would have none of this. Immediately, he withdrew by himself into the hills to pray (John 6:15). This is one example of the many times that Jesus Christ did not do what people wanted him to do unless it was God's will.

Codependency enmeshes with people's feelings and tries to rescue them from their hurts and fix their problems. In contrast, empathy listens carefully to feel people's emotional struggles but never takes responsibility for them. To have empathy for someone is to walk alongside them and support them being accountable to make their own decisions and manage their own lives.

In specific situations of caring for people, there is often a fine line between being empathetic and slipping into codependency. For instance, early in our marriage I (Kristi) had an unconscious tendency to match Bill's mood. If he seemed anxious, I would become stressed. If he seemed angry, I would become irritable. If he seemed depressed, my mood would plummet. I thought I was empathizing with him, but eventually I learned that he did not feel empathy when I matched his mood—he felt pressure to protect me from his distressed emotions.

When we match someone's mood, we are enmeshing with them and losing our separate sense of self. Without the solid base of a self that is differentiated, secure, and esteemed, our capacity to give empathy to others is limited. Empathy is best offered from a place of stability and strength where we can enter into someone's experience in order to understand, not get emotionally swamped, articulate and validate their emotions, and stay grounded in Christ Jesus.

Here is a summary of the key differences to help you identify any codependent (or enmeshing) tendencies you may have and move to the posture of empathy:

Codependency vs. Empathy

CODEPENDENCY	EMPATHY
Feeling someone's problems as your own	Putting words to what someone feels

CODEPENDENCY	EMPATHY
Being controlled by others' needs	Letting others be responsible for their life
Coming from insecurity and low self-esteem	Coming from being secure in God's love
Matching someone's mood or reacting to it	Regulating your emotions as care for another
Denying your own emotions and needs	Accepting your own emotions and needs
Rescuing people from their problems	Showing tender concern for their problems
Trying to make others feel appreciated	Accepting people with no strings attached
Doing too much to help people	Respecting your limits and setting boundaries
Striving to be heroic	Trusting Jesus to provide the ultimate help

Differentiating codependency and empathy in this table helps emotionally drained givers take a look under their hood to see why their engine is not working well. Instead of seeking affirmation for helping other people, we need to work on receiving empathy for our own needs and struggles. This includes naming our emotions, being vulnerable to ask for what we need, and acknowledging our limits. We need to learn to practice the self-empathy of receiving and agreeing with empathy from Jesus and others. Then our empathy and care for others can be healthier.

Carrying Our Own Backpacks

Paul encourages us to "bear one another's burdens and so fulfill the law of Christ" (Gal. 6:2 NKJV). The "law of Christ" is a reference to Jesus' new commandment to "love one another" (John 13:34). Here the Greek word for "burden" means a *heavy weight* that is pressing down on you and is too difficult to keep carrying.[4] It's like trying to carry an enormous boulder. When we are bowed down under the overwhelming weight of a crisis, trauma, health challenge, or grief, we need someone to come along and help us carry our burden. That's what empathy does. It offers a soft and strong heart that comes close with listening, emotional support, and prayer. Empathy sprouts in compassionate actions when we provide a meal, drive someone who is sick to the doctor, or help a student with their homework. Empathy and kindness help us not get buried under a load that's too heavy to carry.

Notice that Paul does not stop with teaching us to bear the burdens of others. He continues, "For each [person] shall bear [their] own burden" (Gal. 6:5 KJV). It seems like a contradiction: "Bear one another's burdens" and "For each person shall bear their own burden." But let's look closer. The Greek word translated as "burden" in verse 5 is different from the word Paul uses in verse 2. This second one means a *light weight* that is part of normal, daily life. It's the same word that Jesus uses to describe his easy yoke as a "light burden" (Matt. 11:30).[5] It's like carrying your own backpack. We get mixed up when we carry other peoples' backpacks for them. They may want to be rescued and let you carry the weight of their responsibilities, but that coddles them and takes away their dignity and opportunity for growth, and eventually it cripples them—and *drains your soul.* We all need to learn to carry our own backpacks, which we can do "freely and lightly" by walking and working with Jesus, who teaches us his "unforced rhythms of grace" (Matt. 11:30 MSG).

Ironically, when you carry someone else's backpack, you'll eventually have to set aside your own backpack or you'll wear yourself out trying to carry both, which is unsustainable. Being overly responsible for someone else usually means you'll be *under*-responsible for yourself, neglecting to deal with some of your own struggles or responsibilities. That's why enmeshing with people and rescuing them is so exhausting—you keep carrying their needs more than your own needs.

Healthy empathy can motivate you to help someone carry their overwhelming boulder for a season without rescuing them. But it does not lead you to carry their backpack for them; instead, you walk beside them as they carry their own backpack, and you give a listening ear and encouragement.

Stewarding Your Empathy

When I (Kristi) burned out with empathy fatigue in my thirties, I learned that I needed to carefully steward my empathy. Now Bill and I have six grandchildren ages seven and under, a family member has cancer, and four other members have mental health challenges. Every day there are other situations in our ministry, family, or friendships that draw on my empathy. That's a lot of empathy output!

Other people's felt needs, especially those of my family, pull on my heartstrings. I can get enmeshed and codependent. I feel the temptation to come to the rescue and be heroic. I think, *Oh, it'd be loving for me to help. Maybe I should do this. I'm probably the only one who can help.* I've learned instead to hold myself back from jumping in to be overly helpful. I've learned to stop and notice how I feel, then think and pray about the situation. *What will this cost me? Do I have it to give? What will it cost others who then won't be able to receive from me because I'm giving my time and empathy to someone else? Lord, is this mine to do? Are you asking me to do this, or maybe you have another way to care for this person?*

Oftentimes, I go a step further and process the situation and my feelings with a friend or my spiritual director, asking for their empathy and prayers. The support I receive strengthens me. It also helps me detach from the situation, de-enmesh from other people's feelings, and discern how God is leading me to steward my empathy and respect my limits. Disentangling myself helps me to see more clearly and to make a more loving decision for everyone involved, including my own self. It helps me to put my faith in God and pray for his ministry to the people I care for.

You can't be empathetic to everyone all the time. If you try to care for others without healthy limits, it'll drain you dry and tax your soul to death. You only have so much empathy to give each day. Instead of letting your tank get empty, you can steward your empathy. You can set boundaries by saying no sometimes, getting enough rest, and putting priority on receiving the empathy you need from a spiritual director or friend. Even our Lord Jesus in his earthly ministry set boundaries for healthy soul care, so you can too!

It's beautiful to shepherd others, but always remember that *first you are a sheep who needs the care of Jesus, the Great Shepherd.* Jesus' great commandment is that we love God first and then love others. But Jesus does not stop there. He does not want us to love others instead of ourselves but love others *as we love ourselves* (Mark 12:30–31). To help us live in the life-giving flow of divine love, Jesus gave us his new commandment to love one another as he loves us, meaning that we are to receive and appreciate his love for us and share it with each other (John 13:34). By relying on Holy Spirit we can become the hands and feet of Jesus, ministering God's empathy and grace to each other.

Notice how Paul stewarded his empathy for the Galatians. Even as their pastor, he asked them to give him empathy as he'd done for them: "Put yourselves in my shoes to the same extent that I, when I was with you, put myself in yours" (Gal. 4:12 MSG). That's *mutual empathy*, which is what you especially need if you tend to overgive to others. He told them that empathy is "sensitive," "kind," "not coming down on" one another, and being "well aware" of one another (vv. 12–13 MSG).

Empathetic Boundaries

When I (Kristi) was a mother of three young adult children preparing to launch into adulthood, I found myself tending to enmesh with their well-being and values. At one point, I was particularly concerned about a problem one of our children was having and was so distressed about it that it was disrupting my sleep. I shared this burden and all my emotions with Bill. He replied that he was concerned too. We prayed together for our child's transition into adulthood. Then Bill remarked, "We've released this to Jesus. We are trusting our Lord and our child, so we can be happy no matter what happens."

Be happy? I was absolutely shocked! This challenged my codependent leaning in that situation. I'd been feeling as if I couldn't be happy without fixing things for our child. Instead, Bill and I learned to walk out the path of empathy with boundaries. We gave our child understanding and care, but we also kept healthy boundaries of practicing self-care and not rescuing them. Trusting the Lord and our child in this way helped us be happy. If we had kept trying to fix things instead of practicing empathetic boundaries, it probably would've hurt our relationship with our child and depleted our own souls.

A pastor of discipleship named Justin needed to learn empathy and boundaries. He had become weary of shepherding people and feeling overloaded with the work of ministry. When someone in his church needed care, he felt he had to say yes. He was prioritizing what others wanted from him but not his own needs. When Justin read our book *Journey of the Soul*, he got language for what he was feeling in his soul.[6] After two decades of pastoral ministry he had burned out in the Responsibilities in Ministry stage of discipleship and hit The Wall. Holy Spirit was drawing him into the Inner Journey stage of discipleship, which meant respecting his limits, being emotionally honest with God and his spiritual director, and practicing new spiritual disciplines like receiving empathy that fostered intimacy with Jesus. Receiving empathy and maintaining healthy boundaries helped him tend to the garden of his soul and be renewed for ongoing ministry to others. For this to be sustainable, he needed sometimes to say no to requests for help and set a limit with empathetic boundaries.

Empathetic boundaries combine empathy for others with setting a limit that respects your own needs. Here are some examples:

"I know you love Mexican food, but it's too spicy for me. Let's find an alternative."

"I hear that you are hurting and need to process. I'm really tired now and not able to listen well. How about we talk tomorrow after lunch?"

"I'm sorry my schedule is too packed to meet till after my vacation. I really want to grab lunch with you and hear your update on how things are going in your new job."

"It seems you are feeling discouraged about this situation, and I want to hear more but I have to get to work. Maybe we can do a part two over breakfast next week?"

Four A's for Empathy Fatigue

Practicing the Four A's of Empathy has helped me (Kristi) to set healthy boundaries in my helping and to stay out of empathy fatigue. Here are some self-empathy prompts to help you prioritize care for your own soul so that your care for others will be healthy.

1. **Ask** questions

   How am I stewarding my empathy?

   Where am I giving too much?

   Who am I rescuing by carrying their backpack?

   What is it costing me to be helping ______?

   What limits do I need to set?

2. **Attune** to emotions

   When someone prevails on me for help, I feel ______.

   While I was caring for ______, I felt emotionally drained.

   When I give so much to people who don't care for my needs, I feel resentful.

   When I listen to the news or read mission appeals, I feel ______.

3. **Acknowledge** the significance

   Not caring enough for my own needs is very dangerous for me.

   My lack of boundaries with ______ is stealing my joy.

   Setting limits with others helps me save energy to love my family well.

4. **Affirm** strengths

I know that God appreciates my willingness to make sacrifices to care for others.

I'm learning important lessons.

Today I took courage and set a boundary with ______.

GO DEEPER

To get free *Deeply Loved* resources, receive empathy from a Soul Shepherding spiritual director, or go on a Soul Shepherding retreat, visit SoulShepherding.org/DeeplyLoved or scan the QR code.

EMPATHY PRACTICE:

Soul Care with Jesus

As a young Christian psychologist and pastor, I (Bill) felt guilty if I set boundaries. I thought I should say yes when people felt they needed something from me. I never wanted anyone to be disappointed or upset with me. It seemed selfish and unkind to say no to people with hurts and needs. But the pressure to care for others depleted me. When I studied Paul's teaching on being a cheerful giver, I realized I had been giving out of compulsion and emptiness and not out of the joy of experiencing God's grace abounding to me (2 Cor. 9:7–9).

After this I was drawn to do a Bible study on Jesus' boundaries. I felt God's empathy for my needs when I saw that even the Savior of the world sometimes said no to people's requests and put priority on his own soul care. His example corrected my distorted view that my first priority was caring for other people. From the human life of Jesus of Nazareth, Kristi and I have received permission and validation to practice healthy boundaries to care for our needs and emotions. Countless people we have helped over the years have greatly benefited from this Bible study. We want you to receive this blessing also.

Learning from Jesus' Boundaries

As you read these examples of Jesus setting boundaries on his ministry, pray for his help to prioritize the soul care you need so that you are sustained in your love for God and people.

Jesus of Nazareth took care of his personal needs for food, water, sleep, and exercise (Matt. 26:20; Mark 1:16; 4:38; John 4:7).

He enjoyed a weekly Sabbath day for worship, rest, and friendship (Mark 1:29; 2:27).

He spent time in nature by the lake, in the fields, in the hills, or in a garden (Luke 4:1–2; 5:15–16; 6:1, 12; 22:39–44).

He was not controlled by people's needs—he left a village when it was time to share the gospel somewhere else (Mark 1:38–39).

He put priority on time to be alone with his Father and pray (Luke 5:16).

He asked those he wanted into a closer relationship (Mark 3:13).

Jesus took naps—even when his disciples wanted his help (Mark 4:38).

He went on retreats with just his closest disciples (Mark 5:37; 9:2; 14:33).

He enjoyed receiving hospitality from his friends (Luke 10:38).

He accepted limits like twenty-four hours in a day and three years of public ministry (John 11:9; 13:1).

The Lord expected everyone he healed to do their part by acting with faith (Mark 6:5; John 5:1–14; 9:1–7).

He did not answer baiting questions designed to trap him but replied with a question or parable (Matt. 9:14–15; 15:1–3; 19:3–6; 22:15–22; 26:6–10).

He did not let his brothers or anyone rush him—he was unhurried as he followed God's leading (John 7:8–10).

He wasn't a people pleaser but was free to disagree with others (Mark 12:35–40).

He walked away from people who had an agenda for him (Matt. 16:4; John 6:15).

Our Savior would not let people throw him off a cliff or stone him to death, because he came to earth to die on the cross for our sins (Luke 4:28–30; John 10:31–39; 12:27).

SOUL TALK

1. What is one lesson on giving too much to others that's important for you to remember?
2. Which dysfunctional family role(s) from your childhood do you relate to?
3. What is a heavy burden in your backpack that you need to set down, at least for a while, to get some rest?
4. What is one takeaway for you on how you can better steward your empathy for others?
5. What is one of Jesus' boundaries or soul care practices that validates something you need?

Conclusion

We are grateful you responded to God's invitation to grow in his grace through empathy. It's been an honor and a joy for us to share with you our stories and life lessons.

You've learned that empathy is feeling with and for someone. In our stressors and hurts we all need to experience three-way empathy from Jesus, ourselves, and others. This requires opening up to your emotions and being vulnerable to ask for empathy from Jesus and safe people. It also requires developing self-empathy, refuting self-judgment and self-rejection by agreeing with and appreciating the grace of empathy. Then you will discover that empathy uncovers sins that need to be forgiven, hurts that need to be healed, conflicts that need to be resolved, and prayers that need to be offered. These are reasons why empathy cultivates deepening intimacy with God and others.

Growing in empathy and its benefits takes time. It'll be helpful for you to keep practicing the Four A's of Empathy (*ask* questions, *attune* to emotions, *acknowledge* significance, and *affirm* strengths) in prayer, journaling, and conversation with friends.

The empathy practices are additional tools for praying Scripture to trust that the Lord Jesus truly feels for you and with you.

What is your next step? How can you continue this journey with Jesus of growing in empathy?

Reading this book with your friends can help you deepen those relationships.

Talking with one of the spiritual directors we've trained offers personalized care.

Attending a Soul Shepherding Institute retreat immerses you in a Jesus-loving community.

Lord Jesus, we thank you for our friend, your beloved disciple, reading this book and for their friends they want to share this journey with. We pray for their growth in receiving and sharing your empathy. We trust you to continue the good work of your Spirit that you've started in them to help them experience your deeper love. Amen.

With thanksgiving and joy,
Bill and Kristi

Acknowledgments

Thank you to the pastors, missionaries, spiritual directors, counselors, coaches, leaders, and students who have shared their stories with us over the years. *You are deeply loved.*

Thank you to our Soul Shepherding board: John and Margaret Snyder, Steve and Joan Graham, Lance Wood, and Steve and Jayne Watts. God uses your prayers, discernment, encouragement, and generosity to fuel our ministry. *You are deeply loved.*

Thank you to our Soul Shepherding staff serving Jesus with us: Sue Wood for directing the staff, Mark Hughes for directing the finances, Kailee Clough and the Marcom team for getting the word out, Amy Dalke for connecting with organizations and leaders who need this book, Briana Holloway for strategic guidance and graphic design expertise, Nicki Bradshaw for helping us manage all our communications and projects, Robyn Jungeblut and the Programs Team for leading the ministry programs, and Dave Rimoldi for shepherding over 150 spiritual direction students and over forty spiritual directors and coaches. *You are deeply loved.*

Thank you to our literary agent, Don Gates, who has guided this project through ideation, writing, publishing, and marketing. *You are deeply loved.*

Thank you to the publishing team at Revell for providing extensive resources: Andrea Doering championed and guided the book, Vicki Crumpton provided inspired and strategic editorial guidance, Amy Nemecek provided clarity in wording and accuracy in numerous details, and Brianna DeWitt and her team provided publicity and marketing support. *You are deeply loved.*

Most of all, thank you to Jesus, our Lord and Savior, the source of divine love, and the Word of God made flesh. *You are deeply loved.*

APPENDIX 1

Empathy Scriptures

Throughout the Bible God offers heartfelt empathy for us, especially through Jesus. The Bible also instructs us to have empathy for one another (as we saw in the empathetic "one another" Scriptures in chapter 4). Below are some of our favorite empathy Scriptures. You may want to highlight the ones that will be helpful for you to come back to for prayer or sharing with a friend.

> The LORD talked to Hagar. She began to use a new name for God. She said to him, "You are 'God Who Sees Me.'" She said this because she thought, "I see that even in this place God sees me and cares for me!" (Gen. 16:13 ERV)

> I have heard your prayer and seen your tears; I will heal you. (2 Kings 20:5)

> The LORD is close to the brokenhearted, and he saves those whose spirits have been crushed. (Ps. 34:18 NCV)

Evening, morning and noon I cry out in distress, and he [the Lord] hears my voice. (Ps. 55:17)

You have collected all my tears in your bottle. (Ps. 56:8 NLT)

The Lord hears the needy. (Ps. 69:33)

As a father has compassion on his children, so the Lord has compassion on those who fear him. (Ps. 103:13)

Because he [the Lord] bends down to listen, I will pray as long as I have breath. (Ps. 116:2 NLT)

In my distress I called to the Lord, and he answered me. (Ps. 120:1 ESV)

Search me, God, and know my heart; test me and know my anxious thoughts. See if there is any offensive way in me, and lead me in the way everlasting. (Ps. 139:23–24)

The Lord is gracious and compassionate, slow to anger, and rich in love. (Ps. 145:8)

"Comfort, O comfort my people," says your God. "Speak softly and tenderly . . ." (Isa. 40:1–2 MSG)

The Lord says: . . . "As a mother comforts her child, so will I comfort you." (Isa. 66:12–13)

God can't heal what you won't feel. (Jer. 6:14, author's paraphrase)

The Lord says, "Listen to the weeping of my people; it can be heard all across the land. . . . I hurt with the hurt of my people." (Jer. 8:19, 21 NLT)

Do to others as you would have them do to you. (Matt. 7:12)

And having felt-deep-feelings [of compassion], Jesus touched their eyes. And they immediately saw-again. And they followed Him. (Matt. 20:34 DLNT)

Moved with compassion, Jesus reached out and touched [the leper]. "I am willing," he said. "Be healed!" (Mark 1:41 NLT)

Jesus saw the hungry crowd and said, "My heart goes out to this crowd." (Mark 8:2 TPT)

Jesus says, "Love others as much as you love yourself." (Mark 12:31 CEV)

Overflow with mercy and compassion for others, just as your heavenly Father overflows with mercy and compassion for all. (Luke 6:36 TPT)

But a certain Samaritan, while traveling, came upon him. And having seen, he felt-deep-feelings [of compassion]. . . . He bound his wounds, pouring on oil and wine. And having put him on his own mount, he brought him to an inn and took-care-of him. (Luke 10:33–34 DLNT)

Jesus wept. (John 11:35)

The Spirit helps us in our weakness. We do not know what we ought to pray for, but the Spirit himself intercedes for us through wordless groans. (Rom. 8:26)

Be happy with those who are happy. Be sad with those who are sad. (Rom. 12:15 ICB)

We who are strong ought to bear with the failings of the weak and not to please ourselves. (Rom. 15:1)

I entered their world and tried to experience things from their point of view. (1 Cor. 9:22 MSG)

I try my best to be considerate of everyone's feelings. (1 Cor. 10:33 MSG)

Praise be to the God and Father of our Lord Jesus Christ, the Father of compassion and the God of all comfort, who comforts us in all our troubles, so that we can comfort those in any trouble with the comfort we ourselves receive from God. (2 Cor. 1:3–4)

Your hard times are also our hard times. (2 Cor. 1:7 MSG)

Put yourselves in my shoes to the same extent that I, when I was with you, put myself in yours. (Gal. 4:12 MSG)

Share each other's troubles and problems. . . . Each of us must bear some faults and burdens of his own. (Gal. 6:2, 5 TLB)

Be kind *and* helpful to one another, tender-hearted [compassionate, understanding], forgiving one another [readily and freely], just as God in Christ also forgave you. (Eph. 4:32 AMP)

[I] feel this way about all of you, since I have you in my heart. (Phil. 1:7)

Therefore if you have any encouragement from being united with Christ, if any comfort from his love, if any common sharing in the Spirit, if any tenderness and compassion, then make my joy complete by being like-minded, having the same love, being one in spirit and of one mind. (Phil. 2:1–2)

Care about them as much as you care about yourselves. (Phil. 2:4 CEV)

Therefore, as God's chosen people, holy and dearly loved, clothe yourselves with compassion, kindness, humility, gentleness and patience. Bear with each other. . . . Forgive as the Lord forgave you. And over all these virtues put on love, which binds them all together in perfect unity. (Col. 3:12–14)

For we do not have a high priest who is unable to empathize with our weaknesses, but we have one who has been tempted in every way, just as we are—yet he did not sin. (Heb. 4:15)

[Jesus, our high priest] is able to deal gently with those who are ignorant and are going astray, since he himself is subject to weakness. (Heb. 5:2)

Be quick to listen. (James 1:19)

[Jesus'] wounds became your healing. You were lost sheep with no idea who you were or where you were going. Now you're named and kept for good by the Shepherd of your souls. (1 Pet. 2:24–25 MSG)

You should try to understand how other people are feeling. Love each other as brothers and sisters. (1 Pet. 3:8 EASY)

Since Jesus went through everything you're going through and more, learn to think like him. (1 Pet. 4:1 MSG)

Above all, constantly echo God's intense love for one another. (1 Pet. 4:8 TPT)

Cast all your anxiety on [God] because he cares for you. (1 Pet. 5:7)

How bold and free we then become in [God's] presence, freely asking according to his will, sure that he is listening. (1 John 5:14 MSG)

APPENDIX 2

Empathy Sentences

Here are some examples of empathy sentences to help you find words for how you or others feel. They are categorized according to the main felt needs we've discussed in this book. There are many statements like these throughout this book, especially in the self-assessments in chapters 6 to 10 and the sections on the Four A's of Empathy at the end of each chapter. You may want to mark the statements below that you relate to and ask a friend to do this so the two of you can share empathy with each other.

Learning to Receive Empathy

In some ways you realize that you have been in an empathy desert.

You long to feel deeply loved by God and others.

It feels vulnerable for you to ask for empathy.

The language of emotions is new for you and you want to learn it.

You really want a close friend so the two of you can share empathy for each other and your love for Jesus.

It warms your heart when you see examples of Jesus' empathy.

Practicing Self-Empathy

You believe you're good at giving empathy to others but not your own self.

It's important for you to learn to resist self-judging and self-rejection.

Practicing self-empathy is new and challenging for you.

It's a comfort to you to see that even Jesus had emotional needs and asked for empathy.

Learning to Give Empathy to Others

It seems you feel inadequate to give empathy to others.

Using empathy skills is new for you and it feels awkward.

It's encouraging for you to learn that empathy is not only emotional but also cognitive.

Caring for others with empathy and prayer feels connective and meaningful to you.

Sometimes when you listen to someone with empathy you feel the warmth of God's presence.

Releasing Worries

It's tiring to be spinning in worry about a number of things.

You're a deep thinker and sometimes you get lost in your head, but you want to connect with others.

It seems you're feeling out of control in this situation.

You feel anxious and scared about what might go wrong.

I see that you're carrying tension in your body and this is tiring for you.

It's encouraging that you're learning to release your worries to God.

Comforting Hurts

You feel like you can't be emotionally real and vulnerable.

It's sad for you that your loved one has not been empathetic toward you.

You've been feeling alone with this issue.

I feel your hurt with you and so does Jesus.

You felt rejected and this feels really sad for you.

Seeing the tenderness of Jesus for hurting people is a great comfort to you.

Calming Emotional Triggers

When you get triggered it's hard for you to breathe.

It's scary for you when you have an emotional trigger.

You're afraid to "lose it" emotionally and be embarrassed.

Gently stroking your face (or asking a loved one to do this) in order to feel Jesus' love is new for you.

Governing Anger with Love

When other people get angry it scares you.

It makes you angry when people put expectations on you.

You feel guilty when you get angry because you don't want to hurt anyone.

Sometimes anger rises up in you and you don't know what to do with it.

It takes courage for you to verbalize your anger and ask for empathy.

Caring for Others Without Getting Drained

You're under pressure to help this person and it's irritating you.

Listening to some people is emotionally draining for you.

I've noticed that when people need your care it's hard for you to say no.

It's encouraging for you to see that even Jesus prioritized caring for his own soul.

When you feel limited in your empathy for others, it's a comfort to pray for them and trust God.

APPENDIX 3

LISTEN Skills

LISTEN is an acrostic for six active listening skills that facilitate empathy:

Loving attitude

Inviting self-disclosure

Summarizing

Timely reflections

Even-tempered

Nonverbal cues

Practicing these six listening skills with a friend or loved one will help you be more effective in giving empathy to others. This is especially helpful when you can solicit feedback on how your empathy was received and what you can do to improve.

Loving attitude

Convey warmth and friendliness: "I'm glad to meet with you."

Be nonjudgmental: "Whatever you need to share, I'm here to listen and pray for you."

Inviting self-disclosure

Ask open questions (not yes-no questions): "How are you? . . . What do you want to share?"

Focus on their emotions: "How do you feel about that?"

Connect their emotions to an example: "What's an example of you feeling that way?"

Go deeper: "Tell me more about that."

Summarizing

Verify their concern: "I'm understanding that you're struggling with ________."

Restate their main need: "It seems you most want help with ________."

Timely reflections

Mirror back their emotions: "It seems you feel ________."

Use fresh words: "My sense is that you're feeling ________. Or how would you describe it?"

Validate the significance: "I can see this issue is very distressing for you."

Identify their personal needs: "I'm hearing that you need more ________."

Go deeper: "In your heart you long to feel the warmth of God's presence."

Even-tempered

Don't react emotionally (e.g., shock, fear, disgust, discouraged, angry). Stay calm and caring.

Keep the focus on their needs and emotions.

Nonverbal cues

Offer a warm smile and soft eyes.

Occasionally nod and vocalize "Mm-hmm."

Scripture Permissions

Unless otherwise indicated, Scripture quotations are from the Holy Bible, New International Version®, NIV®. Copyright © 1973, 1978, 1984, 2011 by Biblica, Inc.® Used by permission of Zondervan. All rights reserved worldwide. www.zondervan.com. The "NIV" and "New International Version" are trademarks registered in the United States Patent and Trademark Office by Biblica, Inc.®

Scripture quotations labeled AMP are from the Amplified Bible. Copyright © 2015 by The Lockman Foundation. Used by permission. www.lockman.org

Scripture quotations labeled CEB are from the Common English Bible. Copyright © 2011 by the Common English Bible. All rights reserved. Used by permission.

Scripture quotations labeled CEV are from the Contemporary English Version. Copyright © 1991, 1992, 1995 by American Bible Society. Used by permission.

Scripture quotations labeled DLNT are from the Disciples' Literal New Testament: Serving Modern Disciples by More Fully Reflecting the Writing Style of the Ancient Disciples. Copyright © 2011 Michael J. Magill. All rights reserved. Published by Reyma Publishing.

Scripture quotations labeled EASY are from the EasyEnglish Bible Copyright © MissionAssist 2018, 2024—UK Charitable Incorporated Organisation 1162807. Used by permission. All rights reserved.

Scripture quotations labeled ERV are from the HOLY BIBLE: EASY-TO-READ VERSION. Copyright © 2014 by Bible League International. Used by permission.

Scripture quotations labeled ESV are from The Holy Bible, English Standard Version® (ESV®). Copyright © 2001 by Crossway, a publishing ministry of Good News Publishers. Used by permission. All rights reserved. ESV Text Edition: 2016

Notes

Chapter 1 Oxygen for Your Soul

1. National Institute of Mental Health, "Any Anxiety Disorder," accessed December 17, 2024, https://www.nimh.nih.gov/health/statistics/any-anxiety-disorder.

2. National Institute of Mental Health, "Major Depression," accessed December 17, 2024, https://www.nimh.nih.gov/health/statistics/major-depression.

3. Centers for Disease Control, "Suicide Data and Statistics," accessed December 17, 2024, https://www.cdc.gov/suicide/facts/data.html.

4. Substance Abuse and Mental Health Services Administration, "HHS, SAMHSA Release 2022 National Survey on Drug Use and Health Data," November 13, 2023, https://www.samhsa.gov/newsroom/press-announcements/20231113/hhs-samhsa-release-2022-nsduh-data.

5. In a survey of more than two thousand US adults conducted online by the Harris Poll in 2022, 43 percent of adults who say they needed care for substance use or mental health in the past twelve months did not receive that care due to many barriers. National Council for Mental Wellbeing, "2022 Access to Care Survey," May 31, 2022, https://www.thenationalcouncil.org/2022-access-to-care-survey/.

6. Brené Brown, *Atlas of the Heart: Mapping Meaningful Connection and the Language of Human Experience* (Random House, 2021), xxi.

7. Kit is not his real name, and identifying details have been changed. This is the case for the other stories of people in this book unless indicated otherwise.

8. You can choose from over fifty Soul Shepherding spiritual directors and about ten Soul Shepherding Institute retreats across the United States or on Zoom at SoulShepherding.org.

9. Six Seconds, "Are We Wired for Empathy?," January 16, 2012, https://www.6seconds.org/2012/01/16/are-we-wired-for-empathy/.

10. Joseph Bryant Rotherham, *Emphasized Bible* (1902; repr., Kregel, 1994).

11. We dropped the word "the" before "Holy Spirit" here and elsewhere to appreciate that Holy Spirit is a precious *name* for the Third Person of the Trinity who is not just a force, as is often thought in our world today, but is a divine Person who loves each of us.

12. In the Common English Bible (CEB) the Greek phrase that is normally translated "the Son of Man" is changed to "the Human One." Here's an example: "Jesus said to them, 'When the Human One is lifted up, then you will know that I Am. Then you will know that I do nothing on my own, but I say just what the Father has taught me'" (John 8:28 CEB).

13. In his incarnation the eternal Son of God chose to set aside his divine privileges and live within the limits of a human body (John 1:14; Phil. 2:6–7; Heb. 2:9, 17). Jesus accepted human limitations (Matt. 24:36; Mark 6:5). When he demonstrated supernatural power, supernatural knowledge, and supernatural love, he said it came not from himself alone but from his perfect faith in God his Father (John 5:19, 30; 8:28; 14:24; Heb. 5:8). As a human being on earth, Jesus loved God and people perfectly and never sinned (1 Pet. 2:22; 1 John 3:5), but he could not love all people everywhere at the same time because he could only be in one location at a time (Mark 1:38–39).

14. In an anxious brain state we breathe fast and shallow, up to thirty times per minute. Mindful breathing is part of a healthy brain state, with our breathing slowing to about fifteen times a minute. Heidi Schreiber-Pan, "Rewire the Anxious Brain," PESI continuing education class, December 9, 2024.

Chapter 2 Jesus' Empathy Finds Us

1. This is a paraphrase of Jesus' beatitudes in Matthew 5:3–10. The blessings that Jesus offers are not based on meeting conditions like being poor in spirit—they are from being part of the Kingdom of the Heavens. For extended teaching on Jesus' beatitudes, see Bill Gaultiere, *Your Best Life in Jesus' Easy Yoke* (self-published, 2016), 58–63.

2. "Kingdom of the Heavens" is capitalized here and elsewhere to emphasize that it is a real place to live. "Heavens" is plural because that is the literal Greek rendering (see, for example, Young's Literal Translation of Matt. 5:3, 10).

3. H. F. Harlow and R. R. Zimmermann, "The Development of Affectional Responses in Infant Monkeys," *Proceedings of the American Philosophical Society* 102, no. 5 (1958): 501–9.

4. H. F. Harlow, R. O. Dodsworth, and M. K. Harlow, "Total Social Isolation in Monkeys," *Proceedings of the National Academy of Sciences of the United States of America* 54, no. 1 (1965): 90–97.

5. "Spirit of Jesus" is another name for Holy Spirit that Paul uses in Acts 16:7 and Philippians 1:19.

6. Travis Bradbury, "Nine Habits of Highly Emotionally Intelligent People," TalentSmartEQ, June 30, 2022, https://www.talentsmarteq.com/9-habits-of-highly-emotionally-intelligent-people/.

7. Aelred of Rievaulx, *Spiritual Friendship*, trans. Mark F. Williams (University of Scranton Press, 2002), 29.

8. *Makarioi* is the Greek word that is repeated in Matthew 5:4–10 and that's usually translated "blessed." It means "happy, fortunate, well off." Young's Literal Translation translates it as "happy."

9. Martin B. Copenhaver, *Jesus Is the Question: The 307 Questions Jesus Asked and the 3 He Answered* (Abingdon Press, 2014).

10. Jesus' compassion is named in Matthew 9:36; 14:14; 15:32; 20:34; Mark 6:34; 8:2; Luke 15:20.

11. Each of these terms is more than an emotion and includes thoughts, bodily states, relational connections, choices, and actions. For instance, love is not an emotion—it is the will to do what is good for others, but it normally includes emotion.

Chapter 3 Self-Empathy Relies on Grace

1. Henri Nouwen, *The Inner Voice of Love: A Journey Through Anguish to Freedom* (Image Books, 1996), 42–43.

2. Angus MacBeth and Andrew Gumley, "Exploring Compassion: A Meta-Analysis of the Association Between Self-Compassion and Psychopathology," *Clinical Psychology Review* 32, no. 6 (2012): 545–52.

3. E. R. Albertson, K. D. Neff, and K. E. Dill-Shackleford, "Self-Compassion and Body Dissatisfaction in Women: A Randomized Controlled Trial of a Brief Meditation Intervention," *Mindfulness* 6, no. 3 (2014): 1–11.

4. K. D. Neff, S. S. Rude, and K. Kirkpatrick, "An Examination of Self-Compassion in Relation to Positive Psychological Functioning and Personality Traits," *Journal of Research in Personality* 41, no. 4 (2007): 908–16.

5. K. D. Neff and E. Pommier, "The Relationship Between Self-Compassion and Other-Focused Concern Among College Undergraduates, Community Adults, and Practicing Meditators," *Self and Identity*, 12, no. 2 (2013): 160–76.

6. K. D. Neff and S. N. Beretvas, "The Role of Self-Compassion in Romantic Relationships," *Self and Identity* 12, no. 1 (2013): 78–98.

7. Quoted in L. B. Cowman, *Streams in the Desert*, ed. Jim Reimann (1925; repr., Zondervan, 2008), 90.

8. Bill and Kristi Gaultiere, *Healthy Feelings, Thriving Faith: Growing Emotionally and Spiritually Through the Enneagram* (Revell, 2023).

9. Empathy Prayer is inspired by Sungshim and John Loppnow, Anna Kang, and Jim Wilder, who developed Immanuel Journaling, a more in-depth process of "interactive gratitude" and "thought rhyming" that they teach in

their book *Joyful Journey*. To learn more, you can also visit the Loppnows' ministry, PracticeAndPresence.com.

Chapter 4 Empathy Loves Others

1. Bill Gaultiere, *Breath Prayer Guides: Renew Your Soul in Bible Verses* (Soul Shepherding, 2019), 21.

2. For more about how to create your own Journey Map, see Bill and Kristi Gaultiere, *Journey of the Soul: A Practical Guide to Emotional and Spiritual Growth* (Revell, 2021), 215–21.

3. See *Healing Prayer: For Emotional and Physical Wholeness* by Bill and Kristi Gaultiere (Soul Shepherding, 2019) for five steps to minister Jesus' healing presence, nine emotionally healing prayer starters, and seven tools for healing prayer ministry.

4. We are taught to "love one another" (or "love each other") in these Scriptures: John 13:34–35; 15:12, 17; Rom. 13:8; 1 Thess. 4:9; 1 Pet. 3:8; 4:8; 1 John 3:11, 23; 4:7, 11–12; 2 John 1:5.

5. Empathy inspires these 58 "one another" or "each other" instructions in the New Testament (NIV): Mark 9:50; John 13:34–35 (3×); John 15:12, 17; Rom. 12:10, 16; 13:8; 14:13; 15:5, 7, 14; 16:16; 1 Cor. 1:10; 7:5; 12:25; 16:20; 2 Cor. 13:11, 12; Gal. 5:13; Eph. 4:2, 32 (2×); 5:19, 21; Phil. 2:5; Col. 3:13 (2×); 1 Thess. 3:12; 4:9, 18; 5:11, 13, 15; 2 Thess. 1:3; Heb. 3:13; 10:24, 25; 13:1; James 4:11; 5:16 (2×); 1 Pet. 1:22 (2×); 3:8; 4:8, 9; 5:5, 14; 1 John 1:7; 3:11, 14, 23; 4:7, 11, 12; 2 John 1:5.

6. First John 4:7 says, "Beloved, let us love one another, because love is from God." Since empathy for others is an important aspect of love, we apply the verse to receiving empathy from God and then sharing that empathy with others.

7. Harper Lee, *To Kill a Mockingbird* (Harper, 2002), 39.

Chapter 5 The Grit and Grace of Empathy

1. Tara Van Bommel, "The Power of Empathy in Times of Crisis and Beyond," Catalyst, accessed December 23, 2024, https://www.catalyst.org/reports/empathy-work-strategy-crisis/.

2. Brian Carbaugh, "The Art of Intelligence," MasterClass, https://www.masterclass.com/classes/the-art-of-intelligence#.

3. Four factors in effective therapy were identified: client motivation, an empathetic relationship, client hope, and therapist techniques. S. C. Whiston and T. L. Sexton, "An Overview of Psychotherapy Outcome Research: Implications for Practice," *Professional Psychology: Research and Practice* 24, no. 1 (1993): 43–51.

4. Henri Nouwen, *Bread for the Journey* (HarperOne, 2006), 65.

5. "Christ and His Friend" is the oldest known Coptic icon. It depicts Jesus and Abba Mena, who was martyred for his faith in Christ in 309. It's currently displayed in the Louvre in Paris.

6. Henri Nouwen, *Lifesigns: Intimacy, Fecundity, and Ecstasy in Christian Perspective* (Doubleday, 1992), 23.

Chapter 6 Releasing Worries

1. American Psychiatric Association, "Americans Express Worry Over Personal Safety in Annual Anxiety and Mental Health Poll," May 10, 2023, https://www.psychiatry.org/news-room/news-releases/annual-anxiety-and-mental-health-poll-2023.

2. Lucas S. LaFreniere and Michael G. Newman, "Exposing Worry's Deceit: Percentage of Untrue Worries in Generalized Anxiety Disorder Treatment," *Behavior Therapy* 51, no. 3 (May 2020): 413–23.

3. *Merimnaó* is the Greek word translated as "worry" in Matthew 6:25–34 (NIV). It's also translated as "anxiety," indicating the Greeks blurred worry and anxiety. *Strong's Concordance*, under "merimnaó," https://biblehub.com/greek/3309.htm.

4. Gaultiere, *Healthy Feelings, Thriving Faith*, 155–65.

5. C. S. Lewis, *The Problem of Pain* (Macmillan, 1962), 10.

6. Helen Pearson, "Nuns Go Under the Brain Scanner," *Nature*, August 30, 2006, https://www.nature.com/news/2006/060828/full/news060828-3.html.

7. *Bay Psalm Book* (1639), original text lightly edited for readability; https://people.sc.fsu.edu/~jburkardt/fun/psalm23/baypsalm.html.

Chapter 7 Comforting Hurts

1. Psalm 69 is quoted ten times in the New Testament to affirm Jesus as the Messiah: verse 4 (John 15:25), verse 9 (John 2:17; Rom. 15:3), verse 21 (Matt. 27:34, 48; Mark 15:36; Luke 23:36; John 19:28–29), verses 22–23 (Rom. 11:9–10), and verse 25 (Acts 1:20).

2. Mother Teresa, *A Simple Path*, ed. Lucinda Vardey (Ballantine Books, 1995), 79.

3. "The Belonging Barometer (Revised Edition): The State of Belonging in America," 2024, https://www.americanimmigrationcouncil.org/research/the-belonging-barometer.

4. The reaction of a startled infant opening its arms is called the Moro reflex.

5. "The righteous cry out, and the Lord hears them" (Ps. 34:17). This same promise of empathy is offered in different words in Exod. 2:24; Pss. 5:3; 6:9; 34:15; 55:17; 145:19; 1 Pet. 3:12.

6. University of Michigan, "Study Illuminates the 'Pain' of Social Rejection," March 25, 2011, https://news.umich.edu/study-illuminates-the-pain-of-social-rejection/.

7. Gaultiere, *Healthy Feelings, Thriving Faith*, 91–102.

8. Emma Young, "Rejection Massively Reduces IQ," *NewScientist*, March 15, 2002, https://www.newscientist.com/article/dn2051-rejection-massively-reduces-iq/.

9. Gaultiere, *Journey of the Soul*, 143–66.

10. There are fifty Gospel readings in Soul Shepherding's *Ignatian Meditation Guides* booklet. These are arranged chronologically and according to the four weeks (or themes) in Ignatius' ancient *Spiritual Exercises*: Our Need for Christ (God's love), Following Jesus (his life and teachings), With Jesus at the Cross, and With the Risen Christ. Each of the three steps in this empathy practice are from this booklet.

Chapter 8 Calming Emotional Triggers

1. Elaine N. Aron, *The Highly Sensitive Person: How to Thrive When the World Overwhelms You* (Broadway Books, 1997).

2. Bianca P. Acevedo et al., "The Highly Sensitive Brain: An fMRI Study of Sensory Processing Sensitivity and Response to Others' Emotions," *Brain Behavior* 4, no. 4 (2014): 580–94.

3. Ronald C. Kessler et al., "Trauma and PTSD in the WHO World Mental Health Surveys," *European Journal of Psychotraumatology* 8, no. 5 (2017), https://www.ncbi.nlm.nih.gov/pmc/articles/PMC5632781.

4. Ekaterina Schneider et al., "Affectionate Touch and Diurnal Oxytocin Levels: An Ecological Momentary Assessment Study," eLife, May 30, 2023, https://elifesciences.org/articles/81241.

5. Aljoscha Dreisoerner et al., "Self-Soothing Touch and Being Hugged Reduce Cortisol Responses to Stress: A Randomized Controlled Trial on Stress, Physical Touch, and Social Identity," *Comprehensive Psychoneuroendocrinology* 8 (November 2021), https://www.sciencedirect.com/science/article/pii/S2666497621000655.

Chapter 9 Governing Anger with Love

1. Josh Wilson, "Cubs Pitcher Broke Hand After Punching Wall When He Was Removed from Game," *Sports Illustrated*, July 7, 2024, https://www.si.com/mlb/cubs-pitcher-broke-hand-after-punching-wall.

2. From a 2006 survey conducted in Britain by *The Sunday Times Magazine*. "Anger Statistics," Mind Your Anger, accessed February 13, 2025, https://www.mindyouranger.com/anger/anger-statistics/.

3. "Boiling Point: Problem Anger and What We Can Do About It" (Mental Health Foundation, 2008), 8, https://www.mentalhealth.org.uk/sites/default/files/2022-09/MHF-boiling-point-report_0.pdf.

4. Heather Murphy, "A Man Demanded His Final Paycheck. The Auto Shop Delivered 91,500 Greasy Pennies," *The New York Times*, March 25, 2021, https://www.nytimes.com/2021/03/25/business/auto-shop-pennies.html.

5. Brown, *Atlas of the Heart*, 222.

6. As recounted in Brennan Manning, *The Rabbi's Heartbeat* (NavPress, 2003), 54–55.

7. Bill Gaultiere, *Jesus' Greatest Teaching: Living the Sermon on the Mount* (Soul Shepherding, 2016), 29.

8. Daniel Goleman, *Emotional Intelligence: Why It Can Matter More Than IQ* (Bantam, 2005). The five EQ traits from his research are self-awareness, self-regulation, motivation, empathy, and social skills. The SMART acronym renames these traits. See Bill Gaultiere, *Emotional Intelligence: 5 Steps with Jesus to Better Living and Leading* (ebook), available at https://shop.soulshepherding.org/.

9. Bernard Golden, "Emotional Intelligence Is a Buffer Against Destructive Anger," *Psychology Today*, April 20, 2023, https://www.psychologytoday.com/us/blog/overcoming-destructive-anger/202304/emotional-intelligence-is-a-buffer-against-destructive.

10. In addition to Psalm 35, some other angry psalms include Psalms 59, 69, 70, and 108.

Chapter 10 Caring for Others Without Getting Drained

1. Leta M. Holder, Beverly J. Farnsworth, and Donna Wells, "A Preliminary Survey of Codependency Traits and Family of Origin Status of Nursing Students," *Journal of Addictions Nursing* 6, no. 2 (1994): 76–80.

2. G. A. Crester and W. K. Lombardo, "Examining Codependency in a College Population," *College Student Journal* 33, no. 4 (1999): 629–37.

3. Cowman, *Streams in the Desert*, 23–25.

4. *Baros* is the Greek word for "heavy burden." *Vine's Expository Dictionary of New Testament Words*, under "burden, burdened, burdensome," https://studybible.info/vines/Burden,%20Burdened,%20Burdensome.

5. *Phortion* is the Greek word for "light burden." *Vine's Expository Dictionary*.

6. Gaultiere, *Journey of the Soul*, 115–66.

BILL and KRISTI GAULTIERE have been counseling and ministering to people for thirty years and are the authors of *Journey of the Soul*. Bill is a psychologist, Kristi is a marriage and family therapist, and they have both served in pastoral ministry. Together they are the founders and leaders of Soul Shepherding, a nonprofit ministry to help people go deeper with Jesus in emotional health and loving leadership. In their Soul Shepherding Institute they offer retreats and a certificate in spiritual direction. They have trained over 350 spiritual directors, and some serve on their ministry staff. Bill and Kristi live in California.

Connect with Bill and Kristi

SoulShepherding.org

A Note from the Publisher

Dear Reader,

Thank you for selecting a Revell book! We're so happy to be part of your life through this work.

Revell's mission is to publish books that offer hope and help for meeting life's challenges, and that bring comfort and inspiration. We know that the right words at the right time can make all the difference; it is our goal with every title to provide just the words you need.

We believe in building lasting relationships with readers, and we'd love to get to know you better. If you have any feedback, questions, or just want to chat about your experience reading this book, please email us directly at publisher@revellbooks.com. Your insights are incredibly important to us, and it would be our pleasure to hear how we can better serve you.

We look forward to hearing from you and having the chance to enhance your experience with Revell Books.

The Publishing Team at Revell Books
A Division of Baker Publishing Group
publisher@revellbooks.com

www.ingramcontent.com/pod-product-compliance
Lightning Source LLC
Chambersburg PA
CBHW070342100426
42812CB00005B/1394
9780800746384